EMERGENT

The Power of Systemic Intelligence to Navigate the **Complexity of M&A**

MIEKE **JACOBS**
PAUL **ZONNEVELD**

RETHINK PRESS

First published in Great Britain in 2019
by Rethink Press (www.rethinkpress.com)

© Copyright Mieke Jacobs and Paul Zonneveld

All rights reserved. No part of this publication may be reproduced, stored in or introduced into a retrieval system, or transmitted, in any form, or by any means (electronic, mechanical, photocopying, recording or otherwise) without the prior written permission of the publisher.

The right of Mieke Jacobs and Paul Zonneveld to be identified as the authors of this work has been asserted by them in accordance with the Copyright, Designs and Patents Act 1988.

This book is sold subject to the condition that it shall not, by way of trade or otherwise, be lent, resold, hired out, or otherwise circulated without the publisher's prior consent in any form of binding or cover other than that in which it is published and without a similar condition including this condition being imposed on the subsequent purchaser.

Cover image © Casther | Adobe stock

Illustrations by Rosi Greenberg – Drawn to Lead

Praise

'This book calls for a new approach to M&A. It's an invitation to confront the unacknowledged questions that so often cripple M&A success. What is the M&A an excuse for? How do we mourn what is lost? Through their questions, Mieke and Paul surface what lies unspoken beneath every system. They name the huge identity shift M&A so often entails. This is a powerful guide to thinking more broadly and deeply about successful integration. Through it, the authors help us begin to identify and understand the constellations in our own organizations.'
— **Jill Ader**, Chairwoman, Egon Zehnder

'A remarkably perceptive understanding of why sensible M&A deals go wrong, and how to get them back on track. This extraordinary work answers a burning question for leaders: "What on earth is happening here, and why?" In every chapter Mieke and Paul pose fascinating questions you haven't asked before, giving you new insights you haven't had before. You will finally understand how your organization really works, and how to help it flourish. Simply brilliant.'
— **Erica Ariel Fox**, *New York Times* Bestselling Author of *Winning from Within: A Breakthrough Method for Leading, Living and Lasting Change*

'Paul and Mieke are two of the leading thinkers in the field of systemic intelligence and organizational constellations. In *Emergent*, they apply their experience and insights to mergers and acquisitions. Through their useful frameworks and real client stories, they provide a window into the underlying dynamics that derail these efforts and offer practical solutions to unleash the full integration potential. Having benefited personally and professionally from the power of their work, and having been touched by their sense of humanity, I will rely upon their wisdom for years to come. I encourage you to place their book at the top of your reading list.'

— **Alexander Caillet**, CEO Corentus; Adjunct Professor, Georgetown University

'I wish I had read this book when I first started working on M&A due diligence and integrations twenty-five years ago. Thinking through the entire process in the systemic way that the authors share with us would have led to much better results.'

— **Jeff Schneider**, Director Strategy Execution, Halyard Health

Dedicated to:

The seven generations that came before us

The seven generations that will follow us

Start Close In

Start close in,
don't take the second step
or the third,
start with the first
thing
close in,
the step
you don't want to take.

Start with
the ground
you know,
the pale ground
beneath your feet,
your own
way to begin
the conversation.

Start with your own
question,
give up on other
people's questions,
don't let them
smother something
simple.

To hear
another's voice,
follow
your own voice,

wait until
that voice
becomes a
private ear
that can
really listen
to another.

Start right now
take a small step
you can call your own
don't follow
someone else's
heroics, be humble
and focused,
start close in,
don't mistake
that other
for your own.

Start close in,
don't take
the second step
or the third,
start with the first
thing
close in,
the step
you don't want to take.

'Start Close In', taken from *River Flow: New and Selected Poems*
Reproduced with permission from Many Rivers Press
© David Whyte

Contents

Introduction

'We trained hard, but it seemed that every time we were beginning to form into teams, we would be reorganized.

I was to learn later in life that we tend to meet any new situation by reorganizing, and what a wonderful method it can be for creating the illusion of progress while producing confusion, inefficiency and demoralization.'
   —Attributed to Petronius Arbiter

Are you willing to:

- Reflect on how you have been handling M&As in the past, and look critically at your strategic plans going forward with a new lens?

- Look beyond what some call 'the madness' of making endless acquisitions without even taking a breath to integrate and stabilize?

- Look in the mirror and understand how you might have contributed to some of the current challenges related to your M&As?

- Live and lead with purpose, looking beyond short-term profits to include long-term sustainability targets and employee engagement?

The target audience for this book includes, but is not limited to:

- The integration teams who work tirelessly to take every integration step in a respectful way

- The men and women who are role modelling, day in day out, a long-term vision and a high value for the human factor in the integration process

- C-suite residents, decision makers in strategic planning, functional leaders with a large stake in the integration synergies (finance, supply chain, logistics, human resources [HR], etc) and operational leaders who will eventually need to make it happen in the field

- Consultants, advisors, team coaches, facilitators who are capable of lending the teams they are supporting time, space, rest, depth and systemic perspective in the heat of the moment

Whether the strategic intent behind the acquisition, merger, divestiture or management buy-out is long-term focused or has a clear short-term objective, we look forward, interacting with leaders who place a high value on an integration strategy and execution plan built on the intrinsic power of the organization and the people beyond the net value of the assets.

In our work with corporations, organizations, teams and leaders all over the world, where M&As are a part of the history and strategic direction, we see tremendous potential to use systemic intelligence to unleash the true integration potential. To sign, seal and deliver a deal that meets or exceeds the objectives in the original business objective letter, not only in the short term, but in all financial, human and societal aspects. To write a company narrative that mobilizes the newly formed organization to achieve and outperform the targets. To ignite or reignite the innovation capacity of the company and manifest a future potential beyond what the founders or leaders dreamed for their company.

One common denominator in our interviews, in our work with large organizations and senior executive teams, and in our thought leadership exchange within our community of transformational thinkers and facilitators is a belief in the critical role of large and small companies in today's world and societies. Leaders need to take full accountability for sustainability and end-to-end thinking in the entire value chain, so it is more critical than ever for them to safe-guard or restore healthy dynamics in organizations.

Needless to say, there is no magical solution to an M&A integration journey. Merging and integrating two $40 billion companies, acquiring a partner much larger in size than you, harmonizing two totally different information and communications technology (ICT) systems, welcoming a corporation with an asset footprint in unknown territory, saving a company from bankruptcy by acquiring it at a low price – all of these are complex challenges. Add to that the magnifying glass of the marketplace and the high monthly or quarterly pressure of shareholders, and integration will always take hard work and tough decisions.

In our work with large and medium-sized corporations, we see integration teams and leaders at all levels going through blood, sweat and tears, putting prolonged peak loads on to both the acquired and the acquiring organization, but not getting the forecasted results. As a result of the increasing resistance in the end-to-end value chain – coming from clients, suppliers, contractors and employees – and lagging KPIs, panic sets in and people start to fight the symptoms instead of addressing the underlying dynamics.

The purpose of this book is not to give you the 'happy pill', the generic medicine that will cure all health problems, but to hand you the instruments to better diagnose the complexity of M&As. To sense, probe, experience and adjust the treatment and recovery plan where needed and identify the elements for a healthy lifestyle going forward. It is tempting to try to codify the rules of the game into a clear textbook or user manual. We call the four principles we will describe in this book the 'natural laws of living systems'. How they are manifested in your specific situation will always require you and your organization to establish relationships within the business you acquire, attune to its system, its history, its key players and its true story, and navigate from there.

Looking at the underlying dynamics with systemic intelligence will allow you to bring the strong invisible undertow to the surface and intervene at the right level, in the right spot, with the right actions. If you don't fully understand what the real root causes are of the problems that you are facing, you risk continuing to face them, or even making them worse. Gaining understanding at the earliest stage possible will save you a significant amount of time and money and may even result in you taking a different strategic course than you'd originally planned.

As a result, you will experience:

- A smoother, faster and more successful integration after a merger or acquisition
- A higher ROI with visible impact on the critical KPIs

- Engaged employees who connect quickly to the new identity, its purpose, values and way of working

- The optimum streamlined design, fit for the new organization

- Increased insights, in-house skills and methodologies to achieve sustainable results, continuously navigating the organization through change and leading in complexity

This book includes first-hand evidence: the experience that we have gained ourselves, the real stories that have been personally told to us, the transformations we have witnessed with our own eyes. Each and every case story is one of our own. Some of those stories are part of our collective memory; others recount our individual past experiences. For ease of reading, we have written those stories from a collective 'we' perspective.

The theoretical foundation is built on systemic intelligence, on the foundational systemic principles and the extensive body of phenomenological experience gained in organizational constellations. It was completed with our experience in large group facilitation, team counselling, executive coaching, trauma in organizations, somatic work, etc.

We dedicate this book to all the men and women out there who find their unique way of expressing passion and care by building strong teams, thriving organizations, profitable companies and sustainable societies.

A True Story:
Immune System

'Our company has a strong DNA,' he says. 'With that comes an equally strong immune system. We immediately push out all foreign elements.'

He, the former Chief Operations Officer (COO) of a multinational $40 billion and 60,000 employee company, is a seasoned business leader, a visionary man. He is enjoying retirement, but he was once the highest-ranked European in the history of this global American-founded corporation. Even though diversity is one of the key drivers of the company's culture, the American roots are strong, as reflected in the nationalities of the executive leaders and the N-1 (those they line manage).

The company history is still visible in its hometown thanks to a museum, and its name is omnipresent in the town's infrastructure and buildings, in its public services. Every employee, and by extension their family, knows the history of the founder. It's a story that is told over and over again.

This is a common trait in long-living organizations. Typically, the founder has a name and a face that's familiar to all employees, and the current values are still connected to some of the founding principles. Remembering and honouring the roots is a prerequisite for the survival of the system. Employees worldwide are bound by this collective memory.

'How is that strong DNA and immune system reflected in the cultural integration phase after an acquisition?'

He smiles. 'You assume that there is a cultural integration.'

He describes the multiple M&As he has been involved in as well-intended and executed with the respectful and gentle touch that is also part of the company DNA.

'But I can guarantee you that it felt like a hostile takeover for the other party,' he adds.

He goes on to tell us that one of the first integration steps immediately after the official signature was always to implant leaders into the newly acquired businesses and sites: leaders who had grown up in the company, demonstrating that they carried the DNA and had the same bloodline. Leaders who breathed the core values, understood how to navigate in the company, knew the dos and don'ts by heart. Strong, competent men and women, yet people who were on a mission to integrate; a mission with a high pressure on time and budget. Mostly, there was little time to really get to know the underlying identity of the acquired business, to patiently listen to the stories that were told there.

The new leaders' mandate was to integrate, find the synergies, implement the best practices and get the return on investment (ROI) as fast as possible – the ROI as expressed in the most obvious key performance indicators (KPIs), specified in the original business objective letter. What they often overlooked was the original strategic intent of the acquisition.

He has also lived through acquisitions where the nature of the new beast was so different that the executive leadership decided from the beginning not to go there, merely adding the new name to the old name in the bottom left-hand corner of all official documents so as not to upset the organization or the customers. Letting the acquired company do business as usual, except for some unavoidable functional processes. No integration; two partners not talking to each other from the very beginning of their relationship.

In the last acquisition under his operational command, he was determined to do it in a different way. The acquired company was still a different beast in an unknown industry, but this time, integration was announced as vital for the future direction of the acquiring company. This acquisition would lead the company into the next strategic wave. It had gone through huge strategic identity shifts only a few times before in its more than 200 years of history.

The technical base of the new partner was fundamentally different, the asset network consisting of a large number of small sites. The client-relationship model, even though some of the client base was shared by both companies, was also fundamentally different. The pride the acquired company felt in its European roots was reflected in the grandeur of the headquarters building.

This time, the acquiring company's intention was to go for full integration while building on the core strengths of the acquired party. Since the knowledge and skillsets for success in this environment clearly differed between the two companies, the acquirer took the decision to leave the current leaders in their positions.

Comparing HR policies showed an interesting difference in the companies' career dynamics. Where one company had a history of fast job rotation, in the other one, the site managers, regional directors and global business leaders seemed to have become attached to their chairs.

One of the site managers clearly understood that the fact he'd kept his position did not necessarily mean that nothing was going to change. He proactively tried to understand the new identity and unwritten rules, but his interpretation was rooted in his own model of the world, so he missed the mark in the implementation. His site had been chosen for the first executive visit, and proudly he raised the American flag next to the previous one. The buyer had always taken pride in being a global company and had never openly given special treatment to the United States.

Despite the positive strategic intentions of the acquirer to honour the acquired company's strengths, even learn from them, adopting their better practices, it almost went wrong in the execution part, with milestones and dashboards, business processes and centre-of-excellence expertise, compliance and company regulations overwhelming the small and previously agile sites. This left the current leaders of the acquired company without a compass to navigate in the new environment.

The entire organization was redirected to an internal focus. That included the sales organization, which brought them to the edge of losing their strong connections to the marketplace.

While he was talking, we could almost imagine the invasion marked with push-pins on a map of the world.

' WE HAVE A **STRONG DNA,**
and **WITH THAT COMES** an EQUALLY STRONG
IMMUNE SYSTEM. WE PUSH OUT ALL
FOREIGN ELEMENTS.'

Questions for reflection

- What is the strategic intent of your merger, acquisition or spin-off?

- Where do you want to be on the continuum, from a holding structure on one end to full integration on the other end?

- What are the consequences of that decision for your organizational design, management processes and performance management?

- What is your strategy for leadership assignments?

- Who benefits from the synergies?[1] Are you planning for a hostile takeover or real cultural integration?

- How can you honour the founders and the founding principles of both parties in the new narrative?

1
Embrace Complexity

'The art of simplicity is a puzzle of complexity.'
—Douglas Horton

When and where is systemic intelligence value-adding and even indispensable? In our work with clients and in open workshops on the use of organizational constellations and systemic intelligence in companies (we will explain both these terms later in the book), we have found that David Snowden's Cynefin framework is helpful to situate it.

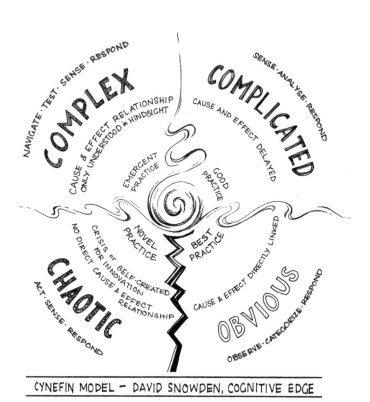

CYNEFIN MODEL — DAVID SNOWDEN, COGNITIVE EDGE

You may be familiar with the expression: 'When you have a hammer, everything looks like a nail'. In the course of our career, we learn and master certain skills, build experience in a specific area, gain insights in numerous professional domains. Often, we recognize the same challenges everywhere we go and apply the techniques we were successful with before. Snowden's model supports us in identifying the characteristics of the situation we are in and defining the right methodology and improvement tools.

We believe that systems thinking and systemic intelligence are indispensable qualities for leaders in this dynamic world, but you might not need to do systemic interventions all the time, and you definitely need other tactics and techniques from your existing toolbox during the pre- and post-merger phases.

'Are we operating in a predictable or unpredictable context?' is Snowden's first question. This is not a single-sided question. We could state that in our current volatile, uncertain, complex and ambiguous (VUCA) world, nothing can be predicted, but even in a broader unpredictable context, there might be areas of predictability.

In his Cynefin framework, Snowden identifies four different contexts.

In the predictable space, he defines two:

- Obvious: where cause and effect are clear and immediate. It is possible to categorize issues and define the ultimate solutions to them. Best practices can be identified and shared.

- Complicated: where cause(s) and effect can be analysed and adequate responses can be identified. Actually, cause and effect might be separated by a time lag or a lack of new insights, but there is still some linearity to be found through analysis. Many seasoned improvement methodologies and tools are perfectly fit for this domain: failure mode and effects analysis, root cause analysis, fishbone diagrams, six sigma projects, etc. We analyse extensively and implement the defined solutions. Given that there are many different variables, these might not be optimal for all, so they are good practices rather than best practices.

In the area of unpredictability, we are talking about:

- Complex: causes and effect seem to be unclear, the system or organization is not responding as predicted, thoroughly analysed solutions and implementation plans are not leading to the desired outcome. We can only conclude that we do not fully understand the dynamics and interconnections; we often only do in hindsight. This is the area where we need to navigate, test or probe, sense and respond. And then we do it all over again, always taking a first step, not a predefined sequence of steps. After that first step, the situation might have changed again, so we need another first step. The visible and invisible interconnections in the system are defined by relation, not by linearity.

- Chaotic: we feel lost and it gets pretty hectic. There seems to be no relation at all between cause and effect. Things are escalating at high speed. People are looking for guidance. The best way to act is to do exactly that: act. We have to stabilize a few things for people to hold on to and observe what is happening. As chaotic as the situation can be and feel, this is also a context that allows for innovation and novel solutions.

Let's take a closer look at the domain of **complexity** as this is exactly where we will apply our systemic intelligence and use our navigation tools.

One of the key questions that always comes up in the leadership forums of Mobius Executive Leadership – the community of transformational leaders and facilitators that we both call 'home' – is: 'Can you, as a leader, hold complexity?' For a long time, a leader's ability to make things simple has been seen as a critical trait for success. In fact, it is often a scoring element in competency-based assessments and development frameworks. It might be useful for a leader to be able to explain complex situations in a clear manner, but applying simple thinking and solutions to a complex problem can aggravate the problem, leading to many unintended consequences.

Instead of making everything simple, ask yourself whether you can see the complexity of a problem and deal with it. Simplifying complex situations holds the risk of overseeing the real issue, fixing the wrong problem, using inappropriate well-known tools and losing the team along the way.

In a similar way, we have tried to apply all the sophisticated analysis tools that are suitable in a complicated context to a complex problem. We analysed the impact of all the root causes we'd identified to the smallest detail, assumed we had found the solution, and were surprised to experience that reality was different.

The nature of complex situations and problems requires us to listen, to watch, to sense. In other words, to think and lead differently. It is probably good enough to analyse to a certain level of detail, to define a solution that's 60% perfect and then start doing something, sensing, probing, testing and experiencing what is happening. That way, we use the systemic principles (which we will examine in more detail in Chapter Three) as a compass, define the right measurement beacons to give us an indication of what is really happening, sense the impact on the organization and respond accordingly. We are often tempted to define a detailed implementation plan with every step marked out, but in complex environments, the situation will have changed after the first step, so the second step might be different to the one we had planned for.

We need different instruments and different qualities to navigate in a complex environment. That is where systemic intelligence and principles come in.

A True Story:
We Missed Ourselves,
So We Bought Them

The company had an impressive track record of acquisitions in its 116-year history, both in size and value. This made the company grow from a local one-person distributor to one of the world's largest in its industry. But the most recent acquisition, two years previously, almost brought it to its knees.

To comply with global and regional monopoly regulations, the company had to sell part of its business portfolio before signature. Some of these businesses were considered to be its crown jewels. Harmonization turned out to be much more challenging than the company leaders had planned for. They didn't realize the synergies, shareholders were losing trust and stock price had gone down to 25% of its value on day zero of the acquisition. Two executives resigned. The company was in crisis.

During our deep-dive session with a small executive task team, we put the timeline on the wall. It went all the way from the first founding principles to the present day and included the foreseeable future. On it, we marked all the important dates and key milestones that had shaped and reshaped the company's identity. It was almost as if we were inviting the founders and the chief executive officers (CEOs) who'd shaped this company into the room.

As we were sharing what we'd heard about the company's culture – being regimented, top down, rigid, detailed to the letter, complex – the vice president with the longest service record sighed and contrasted that image with how it used to be.

'We were entrepreneurial, innovative, forging new paths, shaping the industry. We have invented this industry segment and were the market leaders for decades. We expected leaders to take full accountability and we were known for empowering them and our people. Our M&A strategy has always been to build on the strengths of the acquired companies and give them space, operational freedom and financial accountability. Much of that has been lost, not even that long ago. Maybe ten years ago, maximum.'

This latest acquisition had got everybody excited because the companies had such a similar profile. They were playing in the same field, the cultures seemed close to each other and it looked like a match made in heaven.

'What we didn't realize was that we were not "that" company anymore. We'd lost our identity along the way.'

As the vice president spoke her next words, we heard probably the most beautiful sentence ever related to M&A work:

'We missed ourselves, so we bought them.'

' WE MISSED OURSELVES
SO WE BOUGHT THEM. '

Questions for reflection

- What is the historical timeline of both parties? What are critical events that have defined each company's identity?

- What are the founding principles of both companies?

- What is the history of leadership in the acquired company?

- Who was the last leader that was considered successful?

- What is this M&A an excuse for? Which dimensions, characteristics, qualities, strengths are you trying to buy because you lack or have lost them?

2
The Sobering Reality

'The Hour shall not occur until the Euphrates will disclose a mountain of gold, over which people will fight. Ninety-nine out of every hundred shall die, and every one of them shall say: "Perchance I shall be the one to succeed".'
—Islamic and biblical prophecy

Setting the stage

Different sources measuring, evaluating, commenting on and predicting our global economic dynamics indicate that between 70% and 90% of all M&As will fail.[2] At the same time, without exception, they confirm that in the years to come, both M&A deal activity and deal size will continue to increase.

How do we define 'failure' in this context? The most obvious way would be to look at financial measures, comparing additional shareholder value before and after the deal. KPMG's global research report on M&As reveals that only 17% of merger deals boosted shareholder return.[3] The stock market might show an initial positive response to inorganic growth announcements from CEOs shaking hands in front of the camera, but the longer-term reality shows a different picture.

From a systemic point of view, we are extending the measures of failure based on what we see daily, even years after the acquisition date:

- Failure to write a convincing new narrative that includes both companies' legacies

- Failure to engage the acquired organization in the narrative and company values

- Failure to retain talent

- Failure to build a strong and agile organizational structure that is far beyond a compromise

- Failure to root the new culture in the past, so that it has a longer lifespan

- Failure to respond to changing market dynamics or bold moves from the surrounding systems

- Failure to resolve longstanding issues that date back to the acquisition, or even further back in time

- Failure to harvest the full potential of the acquisition

How to measure success

A BCG survey among corporate leaders revealed that 64% of them measure the success of all their acquisitions, while 34% do it only for what they consider to be the important deals.[4] Criteria that these leaders measure against most often:

1. Improved profitability

2. Revenue growth

3. Milestone tracking

4. Synergy tracking

5. Shareholder value

Interestingly enough, the BCG survey demonstrates that most companies have standardized processes in the deal preparation and execution phase, such as target search, decision making, team formation, due diligence and valuation. When it comes down to the finalization phase, though – those critical post-merger integration weeks, months and years – the 64% of leaders measuring the success of all their M&As goes down to 39%. But wouldn't that be the most important part of the journey to safeguard a smooth transition for clients, assure a strong launch in the market and ignite an energy boost in the organization?

In the scope of this book, we suggest adding stakeholders and elements to the list of criteria, as we believe that they are critical to achieving the desired profitability, growth and shareholder value. Let's take a look at the post-merger impact on the customers, employees and asset network and gauge the M&A success from their perspective.

The customer

'Customer-centricity' is often one of the core values of one or both parties in a M&A, but the importance of existing and potential customers can be overlooked in the immediate post-merger phase. Research and experience show that customers are not benefiting at all from M&As.[5] They are left confused and unclear about the price impact of the companies' combined product portfolio. They are faced with new contacts in the sales force and have to re-establish relationships with representatives who may not be equipped with the overarching storyline and the necessary skills to represent the merged companies' offering.

Because of the high workload of post-merger integration plans in the areas of systems, procedures and management processes, the entire new organization can sometimes turn inwards and adopt an internal focus – until the market starts to complain. By then, the organization's market share is in rapid decline, and recovery plans are often cumbersome, leading to irreparable margin losses.

The employees

Identified synergies will mostly lead to pre- and post-merger restructuring and fixed cost-cutting programmes with fancy names like 'Repositioning for Growth' or 'Career Transition Plan'. While this is often accounted for in the financial plan as a bottom-line one-off restructuring cost, the actual costs are much higher.

The first employees who are typically included in the lay-offs are the people who are closest to retirement, even if that is still ten years away, which results in a loss of critical experience. In knowledge-intense industries, guarding technology, operational expertise and years of troubleshooting experience is critical, and the effect of losing it all at once is often only visible in the mid-term as process problems arise.

Additional loss of vital experience and skills occurs when high-potential employees decide for themselves to leave. Exit interviews we conducted with people about what led to their departure revealed some common themes:

- No clarity about roles, responsibilities and career growth potential in the newly formed company

- The impact on the organization of unhealthy and unproductive power battles between senior executives

- Prolonged integration workloads without tangible and intangible recognition

- Lost connection with the marketplace

- Forced top-down implementation of common corporate practices not suitable for the specific industry, segment or business-unit needs

But most of all, the people who chose to leave indicated that they 'didn't feel it anymore'. The founding spirit or core values that attracted them to the organization in the first place had been lost and they couldn't buy into the story and the purpose any longer.

'It's simply not the same company anymore' is a complaint we've heard time after time, and of course, it isn't. It will never be the same company again, so how can we ensure that people find their way in the new organizational system and connect to the new corporate and team identity?

This question brings us on to probably the most important group of employees: the people who are staying. In an attempt to assure a fair exit for the ones who have lost their jobs, company leaders often give little attention to the men and women they actually want to excite with the new vision. These employees need the space to go through a mourning phase before they can adjust to the new rhythm and embrace the merged identity. Depending on the strategic intent of the merger or acquisition, the employees of the buying party might feel equally insecure about their position and role in the future organization, especially when the acquisition is presented as the first step in *the* new strategic wave or being vital for the company's future.

As the integration overload can be intense, it may lead to serious distractions during the early phase, not only in the functions, but also in the plant sites where the integration efforts of all functions come together for implementation, with limited prioritization. This overload keeps leaders and influencers away from their teams and from the shop floor.

The assets

On top of a merger of people, in most M&As, we are also talking about a merger of assets, often the most tangible part and biggest liability in the whole deal. A company's asset footprint, be it manufacturing plants, natural resources, properties, facilities, distribution fleets, real estate, etc, can change drastically after a merger or acquisition.

As the due-diligence phase is mostly stretched in terms of time and budget, restricted by confidentiality agreements and focused on many business performance indicators in parallel, and as the 'courted' family is sometimes dressing up the bride, the acquiring company doesn't always have the complete picture of the actual condition of the assets, the operational reality at the sites and the robustness of the management processes until the ink is already on paper. Despite the strategic synergies, the different parties and their assets can have different profiles, meaning that a one-size-fits-all approach won't lead to the right results, and may even cause performance and maturity to deteriorate.

What we often experience is that sites with a long-standing maturity in culture and management processes all of a sudden make a backward loop and revert to an old style and behaviour. The two parties may be using different operational definitions for KPIs, leading to difficulties in aligning them to one harmonized reporting structure. This means that visibility on the actual performance of the combined company reduces for quite a while, so sites don't pick up the leading signals that performance or culture is actually deteriorating.

It is not within the scope of this book to explore the state of assets or the age and reliability of manufacturing sites and production lines, nor to evaluate the net present value of equipment or real estate. We will come back to assets later in the book, though, as a few of the systemic principles we will outline will definitely apply.

In this chapter, we briefly identify with the employees and customers who are impacted. On top of that, if you were to look at the corporate world beyond the direct stakeholders, through the lens of societal value, corporate social responsibility and true sustainability, you might see an additional cost of failure that is significant but partly hidden.

Critical success factors

Several consulting firms and business publications have formed their opinion about the critical success factors for increasing your chances of being in the desirable top 10 to 30% of successful industry leaders. EXL[6] identifies and quantifies the key success factors for an M&A:

- Integration planning 39%

- Cost valuation 31%

- Due diligence 18%

- Economic environment 11%

- Others 1%

Integration planning being the number one success factor in this list doesn't necessarily imply a post-merger integration (PMI) that focuses on resolving the real underlying challenges and unleashing the full potential of the organization.

PwC[7] identifies four critical success factors and includes a reference to the human element:

- Project governance
- Synergies
- Speed of integration
- Culture and change management

Is this culture and change management approach aimed at absorbing the newcomers into the dominant acquiring culture, or is this post-merger moment recognized as a unique opportunity to redefine the purpose of the entire organization, its structure, its values, culture and modus operandi?

To quote a McKinsey study around culture:

> When the CEOs in a deal get along with each other, they tend to assume that their companies will get along equally well. No two companies are cultural twins, and companies seldom get along with each other as easily as their executives might.[8]

Oliver Wyman's extensive experience with M&As nails it down in this statement:

> 'The soft factors determine success.'[9]

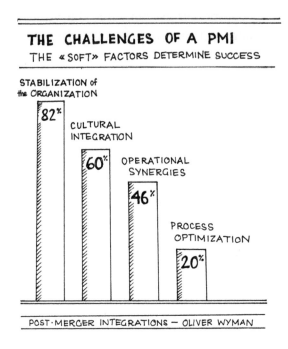

THE CHALLENGES OF A PMI
THE « SOFT» FACTORS DETERMINE SUCCESS

STABILIZATION of
the ORGANIZATION

82%

CULTURAL
INTEGRATION

60%

OPERATIONAL
SYNERGIES

46%

PROCESS
OPTIMIZATION

20%

POST·MERGER INTEGRATIONS — OLIVER WYMAN

What if we didn't consider stabilization of the organization and cultural integration as 'soft', but rather as visionary, foundational and of strategic importance?

Merging two companies in alignment with monopoly regulations, multiple countries' legislation and financial conditions; identifying synergies in multiple technical domains; and ensuring that financial targets are met is indeed a complex undertaking which is beyond the scope of this book. We are aiming to add an additional dimension to it that dives into the deeper systemic layer, which is potentially the one that makes the difference between failure and sustainable success. On top of all the text-book checklists, the pre- and post-merger assessments, the implementation templates with multiple swim lanes, we would like to add more systemic questions:

- What is this M&A an excuse for?

- What are you really trying to buy?

- What were the original founding principles of both parties?

- What will the true purpose of this newly formed company be?

- What does your organization want to be? A holding company or an integrated unit? What are the consequences of that decision for your organizational design, management processes and performance management?

- What is the new narrative? How do you include both companies' narratives and histories in it?

- What is the new order of things?

- What is the place of every business unit, department and individual in the future?

- What will the pecking order be based on in this new system?

- What gets lost in this deal?

This seems like the right moment to dive into systemic intelligence and introduce you to the systemic principles, which we'll look at in the next chapter.

A True Story:
Somatic Scars

'I still feel the somatic scars of that acquisition,' he says, even though almost twenty years have passed since.

'Where in your body do you feel that?' we ask him. He points at his chest. The acquisition was literally heart-breaking.

He joined a visionary consulting firm as a young psychologist. The firm was on a high at the time and had a track record of impressive productivity results by creating shared services with major clients. The founder was a man with a legendary personality and consciousness. He gathered like-minded partners, consultants and associates around him and took them along on his visionary journey. They did groundbreaking work, forged new paths, were not bound by conventional consulting approaches.

It was highly exciting – until the founder drove it to the edge. He was running too far ahead, which opened the gateway for some underlying mutiny on his ship. Several partners felt that his personal journey was interfering with their professional mission and that their internal community focus was diverging from the business case at a client level.

In an off-site visionary session, the executive team opened the door for a takeover by another consulting firm that had been courting them for a while. Financially, it would be interesting for all partners, and they enthused the juniors with a share in the deal. The founder would stay on board as a senior advisor, which comforted part of the organization, but it turned out to be of short duration. Two captains on one ship – it has seldom worked out well. The cultural clash between the innovative and inspiring small player and the disciplined and number-focused major player was huge.

'We went from dancing to marching,' he tells us.

One year after the acquisition, all of his team had left the company, taking their client relationships with them. The acquiring company stayed behind with an empty shell.

'WE WENT FROM DANCING to MARCHING.'

Questions for reflection

- Have you really evaluated the compatibility of the two cultures?

- Are personal financial drivers blinding the decision makers?

- Which tough decisions are you avoiding for the sake of false harmony?

- What needs a real ending, who needs a proper farewell, so that there can be a new beginning?

3
Looking At All Parties With Systemic Intelligence

'El rio abajo el rio.'
—Clarissa Pinkola Estés

Setting the stage

El rio abajo el rio – the river underneath the river. Maybe there are even multiple rivers underneath the river.

How many of you are fighting symptoms on a daily basis? Trying to resolve issues that seem to have no logical explanation, no obvious source or no clear root cause?

Systemic dynamics are the invisible winds that blow through a company. Sometimes they give a team wings to enable its members to fly. More often, though, they feel like a storm roaring on to the shore, deciding what needs to be destroyed along the way. That is why thinking, working, leading and being systemically aware is a much more effective way to reveal the patterns and underlying connections in an organizational system.

Systemic intelligence surfaces the roots of seemingly intractable 'stuckness', illogical resistance to change, persistent roadblocks and disappointing results.

Systemic intelligence

This expression might trigger mental models in you, like artificial intelligence versus human intelligence, emotional intelligence or secret intelligence. Maybe systemic intelligence is actually a combination of all of that, and more.

OPERATIONAL DEFINITION:
SYSTEMIC INTELLIGENCE

A way of living where you relentlessly strive to understand the whole, the parts and their interdependencies. You are always willing to consider the upsets and challenges as symptoms of something you might not see yet and you are eager to unravel the real maze. You are considering your own place and role in the system, and with that the opportunity for real change and transformation.

In practical terms, it implies that you apply the four systemic principles of purpose, connection and inclusion, order and occupying one's place, and exchange, and their many manifestations as a lens for learning and understanding.

Systemic intelligence is a combination of the competencies, beliefs, knowledge and experience of many. It summarizes accumulated wisdom, gathered over many years in the domain of constellations and systemic work. Below is a non-exhaustive list of what it means for us to journey through life – whether it is the corporate world, our own family, community or society – with systemic intelligence.

It starts with 'seeing systems'

When we first introduce the concept of organizational systems, it often takes some time for people to let go of their mental model of what a system is. We are not talking about an advanced operating system, the new information technology (IT) or HR computer system, or any other technical software or set-up.

OPERATIONAL DEFINITION: A SYSTEM

A set of interacting or interdependent entities forming an integrated whole. Those interdependencies are often happening on an unconscious level and are therefore invisible. A system is subject to natural principles or laws. It attempts to maintain its integrity and restore its dynamic balance by making corrections to realign with internal and external forces.

If the system is not achieving its purpose, instead of pushing it even harder, we need to become really curious to understand what is going on with the interacting parts and their interdependencies. Systems simply don't tolerate 'moving on', 'forgetting' or 'excluding'. They will employ correcting mechanisms and entanglements until the real issues are attended to.

Teams, departments, business units, companies and, by extension, the value chain and community they are operating in, are actually living systems.

Recommended read

Arie de Geus describes these dynamics in his 1997 book *The Living Company: Habits for survival in a turbulent business environment*. According to de Geus, all corporations are built on two hypotheses: 'the company is a living being' and 'the decisions for action made by this living being result from a learning process'.

Peter Senge offers us 11 Laws of Systems Thinking in his book *The Fifth Discipline: The art and practice of the learning organisation*: 'Systems thinking is a framework for seeing interrelationships rather than things, for seeing patterns of change rather than static snapshots.'

Nothing works in isolation. All elements in an organization – people, departments, process steps or product characteristics – are visibly and invisibly connected to each other. Systems are not simply defined by their elements, but by the relationships between them. Understanding and influencing the interrelations is critical to achieving the desired outcome. If the outcome is not what you intended, you need to explore the entire system and the underlying dynamics, not just fight the symptoms.

Doing so requires a different lens and a deeper knowledge of systemic principles, as the underlying dynamics are seldom explicit. Rather they are implicit or show up in disguise. The symptoms are visible on the surface, but we will have to reveal the forces underneath, the undertow that is stronger than our well-intended implementation plans.

It's not about knowing; it's about navigating

An experienced sailor will have planned their journey to the last detail. They will have all their parameters set before they raise the sails and head into the direction of their destination. But then the current throws them off track.

The current in a river or an ocean is invisible, fast, strong and unpredictable. It is also what will carry you to ride the waves, if you find it and respect it.

The systemic principles of purpose, connection and inclusion, order and occupying one's place, and exchange, which we will cover in detail in the next chapter, can be used to scan the horizon. They will help you to check all sounds on the ship (your organization) for subtle shifts, be the compass that keeps you on course to constantly navigate in unknown waters and support you in defining the next 'first step' when the direction of the wind changes.

It is not easy to step out of the cycle of analysing, predicting, planning, launching, implementing and executing. Many companies operate in high-risk industries where risk management, scenario planning and full control of critical processes are vital for their license to operate. We are not suggesting you let go of that, but that you are willing to let go of your inner protocol, your assumptions about how things are supposed to go. The strategy that worked to fight the same battle last time will not necessarily work now.

As consultants, coaches, facilitators, we are not spared from some form of attachment to a desired outcome. It is tempting to recognize the well-known dynamics from companies we've previously worked with in a new situation, to choose proven methods and interventions over not knowing. Yet there is no other way if we want to explore the full potential of systemic work.

Perpetuum mobile

We started this book with David Whyte's poem, which reminds us to 'take the first step'. It is a dynamic world; the optimal solution will often be outdated before we have even implemented it. We often see plans for a two-year improvement journey, for a detailed integration implementation roadmap with monthly milestones, but in the M&A environment, the combined organizational system might react to your first moves in a totally different way than you expected. So the second step you had planned might not be the right one anymore. You might have a detailed plan in mind, but it is more important to take the first step and experience how the organization reacts to it, process the impact, understand what to conclude from it about your initial assumptions and the interconnections, and adjust your next move accordingly.

There is a consideration to make here. If you are leading a large organization, there is a need for stability – 'consistency to purpose' as one of our clients called it. Employees express a need to understand the direction, buy into the tactics and stick to the plan, at least for a while.

At the same time, there is also a need to shift to a 'failing fast' culture. In these VUCA times, it poses a real risk to hold on to outdated plans, to not stop a project because you have already spent money and resources on it. It might seem easy to deny that the workforce is reacting totally differently than you expected – it is hard to admit that some of your decisions turned out to be the wrong ones, but in the end, it's what you must do.

It is still important to set a clear direction, draft a plan and define the operating boundaries. Just realize that the road might not look like the one you mapped out.

How to see both the forest and the trees

A company is a multi-layered, tangled web of many systems. At every moment, it forms a system in itself, designed to achieve the vision and mission as defined in its three- or five-year plans. It is interacting with its environment through the value chain, connecting customer needs to its products or services, and purchasing raw materials, natural resources, or knowledge to produce or deliver them. Within every corporate organization, a well-thought-through and sometimes highly dynamic design defines how the company is structured and how business units, departments, teams of people are contributing to the goals, each of these forming a system in itself. This is called the organizational system. It has all these subsystems attached to it.

Whether it spans a few decades or even centuries, or is a newborn startup, every company is built on the first idea of the founder(s) and is still influenced by it. This founding spirit represents the beginning of the organization; the originating system; the breath that blew life into the first manifestation of the company it is today.

The human capital, as it is often described, consists of employees at all levels. This capital, formed by individuals and the relationships between them, can be laid over the organizational system and interact with it. When entering the door, when signing a contract of employment, each individual brings in dynamics and beliefs from their own family system. On top of that, challenging dynamics or 'unsolvable' problems might date back one or two generations or be connected to a seemingly unrelated event.

To start detangling this complex mix of systems, interconnections and dynamics, it is essential to identify the relevant system for a specific challenge or problem. One of the most important qualities in systemic intelligence is to be able to discern what belongs where. There is good news if you are willing to let go of the desire to intellectually master complexity and use all your additional senses and innate resources.

Stop talking and use your senses

In our combined forty-five-plus years of experience in industry, consulting and coaching, we have both come to realize that our road to higher clarity is characterized by letting go of whatever is redundant. Endless spreadsheets with analysis, theoretical discussions, intellectual frameworks and models, and many hours of talking are unnecessary when you listen for core language; when you look for the river beneath the river; or when you create a visual representation of the situation and let it reveal the dynamics that are masked by the problems on the surface.

CASE STUDY: TABLEAU VIVANT

We ended a diagnostics day with a 'constellation', a felt experience of the real dynamics. We positioned an object that represented the change programme in the middle of the room and asked each of the different team members to represent one group of critical stakeholders and find their position in relation to the change programme.

The *tableau vivant* was revealing. Where one department was almost standing on top of the object, their attention focused on nothing else, other departments were observing from a distance, sitting on the floor or even standing on the table, looking down at it. The constellation showed us a disjointed system with a broken chain of command and a disparate layer of middle management, which explained the employees' contrasting opinions and beliefs about the transformation ahead.

All participants confirmed afterwards that this half hour had been most impactful and opened their eyes to the real dynamics. It gave them a different perspective on what to do next, which led to a much more integrated tactical implementation plan.

In our work with executive leaders or integration teams, we often use constellation techniques both as a diagnostic tool and as an intervention method. If you are not trained in these techniques or feel uncomfortable facilitating a full constellation, we will provide you with some ready-to-use tools and techniques that will give you an immediate perspective on the systemic dynamics.

Less is more

Letting go of redundancy also applies to the actions, solutions or interventions you identify. As you are operating on a deep level, a small intervention will have a big impact.

You may have tried to engage the acquired organization's employees many times with big communication campaigns, town-hall meetings, extra incentives or bonuses, but they still reject the new reality. Finding out the origins of the rejection might show you that it only requires a relatively small intervention to bring them on board. After an M&A, the acquiring partner sometimes simply needs to acknowledge that this acquisition date is not just another snapshot on their timeline; that this acquired partner, additional business unit, site or bunch of employees did not just fall from the sky.

We have worked with merged companies where the CEO position has been filled four or five times in a short time span. Executive search partners were scratching their heads, trying to find the next candidate, but understanding what was really 'contaminating' the CEO chair was what they really needed to be doing to interrupt this repetitive cycle. We have witnessed various sources of contamination: the founding CEO leaving his chair but keeping an office next door, the previous CEO being dismissed one day because of fraud, a number one executive who was seen to have abandoned the ship just before a crisis, and many others.

The system is stronger than the individual

Stay with us for a moment, even if this statement isn't landing with you right away. In essence, what any living system wants to achieve is survival. To do so, it will restore harmony on a deeper level even if that means creating what may look like destructive dynamics.

What does it feel like when there is harmony and energy flowing in an organization? Employees are excited about the company vision, results are visible, people go the extra mile to achieve a stretch target. Innovative ideas are welcomed, turnover and absenteeism are low, there are opportunities for growth and personal development, teams are collaborating towards one common goal.

Most probably, you know the opposite situation all too well. But what may look like the disturbing behaviour of individuals or groups, what may sound like mutiny or feel broken and dysfunctional, can be the symptoms of a restoring mechanism.

How often do organizations remove individuals who are considered uncooperative only for the next opposer to stand up and demonstrate the exact same behaviour? What if those organizations were to consider their employees' opposition as a warning signal? A symptom of something more fundamental, something that we do not yet see?

We worked with an organization that had introduced an additional customer care department following shareholder feedback that the customer-service level was below expectations. You may think that was the right thing to do, but would you still feel the same if we were to tell you that there was already a hardworking and dedicated customer-service team in place? Customers reacted positively to the extra attention they got from the customer care department on top of their existing relationships with the customer-service representatives, but it created a complete disruption in the internal system.

The highly skilled and engaged customer-care leader was exhausted. On her own initiative, she had started a coaching journey to work on her leadership skills and impact. She initiated reconciliation efforts between different departments and engaged the members of her own team, but none of her well-intended actions resolved the issues.

The system is stronger than the individual. As long as underlying restraining forces are invisible, you will only be fighting the symptoms. The strongest leader, the most well-intended operational manager, the most highly skilled expert will not be able to overcome what is in reality a misunderstood, distorted system. You can restore harmony and flow only when you become aware of and respect the principles or natural laws of systems.

Recommended read

A fascinating read about the innate wisdom of the system is Humberto Maturana and Francisco Varela's *Autopoiesis and Cognition: The realization of the living.*

In the beginning, there was nothing

It is critical to honour the origins and understand the history of an organization. Every organizational system starts with an idea the founder had, maybe long before he or she signed the statutes of the company. We are talking about the intention or desire that preceded the actual conception – the innovative spark; the brilliant or creative idea; the insight or burning ambition to change something or add value; the determination to improve. What defines the colour and culture of this first version of the company is a willingness to manifest the founding idea and take the risk that comes with it.

In our work with M&As, we will always include the timeline of both parties to fundamentally understand the founding spirit of each, to consider the key milestones that marked their growth or identity shifts, and by doing so we'll honour what can add value going forward.

What it takes

Embracing all of these ideas requires some new competencies from you as a leader or advisor. This is not just another model or analytical tool; it's an attitude with a set of skills, beliefs, mindsets and behaviours that, once embraced, will keep evolving and expanding into uncharted territory. We will outline here what it requires from leaders, change champions, programme managers, facilitators and consultants. This is a list that we keep extending along the way.

It demands a new way of listening

If you have ever seen movies of Dan Brown's books, starring Tom Hanks in the role of Professor Robert Langdon, you might remember that the professor has an eidetic or photographic memory. In the movie scenes where he is using this, it's portrayed as if letters, words or symbols are jumping out, forming a new combination in front of his eyes and giving him the hidden answer.

In a way, this image illustrates systemic listening. As you can imagine, after many years of working on and listening for the impact of M&As, we have both developed an M&A 'sixth sense'. In this book, we will offer you systemic questions to help you listen out for different words and statements. When you learn to listen using all your senses, there is no going back. You will start seeing systems and systemic alerts everywhere.

The more you pay attention, the more you will notice that some words or sentences almost seem to have another colour. We call this core language. Which words or sentences stay with you or seem out of place? Those are the clues and cues you need to become aware of, pick up and pursue.

Deal with ambiguity and not knowing

Everyone is tempted to use their knowledge and hard-won wisdom, but we will sometimes ask you to let go of everything you know and be open to a new possibility. We want to invite you to walk into a familiar field with genuine curiosity and trust what the system is telling you. There is no one-size-fits-all manual. The systemic principles we will describe in the next chapter are reconfirmed again and again as universal principles in living systems, but their actual manifestation in each situation requires a closer look, the willingness to be surprised. We have to relate to every new system, to every team and leader again and again as if it is the first time.

Remember that you have a body

We tend to think of our brain as the magical tool for observation, analysis, processing and decision making, but our physical analysis instrument actually looks more like this.

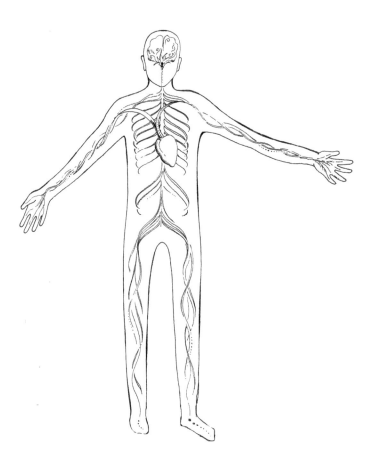

Our body is a refined instrument that will give us much more information if we are willing to tune it on a regular basis and listen to its sounds and resonance. Systemic work requires full presence, body awareness, increased perception and observational skills, and what we call embodied wisdom. Pay attention to your own and other people's energy levels, bodily sensations, movements, breaths or sighs. Goosebumps might tell you that you are on to something; a lurch of the stomach may urge you to better understand the source of tension in the room. Being totally exhausted at the end of a full day of integration work is perhaps an indication of the lack of vitality in the team, and by extension in the entire organization. Without jumping to conclusions or interpreting these additional indicators, learn to trust them and pause your team on a regular basis so they can observe what is happening. Your brain will still get a seat at the table, but so will your entire nervous system.

So far, we have explored what we mean by organizations being living systems with deep layers of connections and interdependencies between all the parts and players involved. We've had a look at our understanding of what systemic intelligence is and what mindset shifts it requires. In the next chapter, we will share with you our navigating principles and how they show up in organizations, specifically in M&As.

A True Story:
The Customer... Who?

We are talking to the global marketing director. 'We got it right the third time,' he says.

In a timespan of a few years, he has lived through two acquisitions and is now in the aftermath of a spin-off. What he actually means by his statement is that the organization finally got it right for their customers.

'In the very first one that I was involved in, we were focused on simplicity. At least for ourselves.'

In hindsight, it is crystal clear to him that by minimizing the internal transition effort, the organization had transferred all the burden to its customers.

'It was easy for us, and hell for them.'

Instead of assuring the customers that this strategic decision would benefit them, and that the organization would safeguard a smooth transition, the executive team had imposed all the systems, portfolio, pricing and contact changes on to the customers. They presented them with a thick manual containing the transition guidelines and future way of working.

'I can tell you, we paid the price for it,' he says. Communication campaigns failed, critical updates were rejected, transactions went wrong because of wrong information. Mostly, customers were upset, complained or ran away. As they didn't trust supply reliability anymore, they were adding buffer orders, so the organization's forecast became totally distorted. He describes the internal atmosphere as a war zone, everybody blaming one another for the disastrous customer experience. It took the organization a long time to stabilize the situation.

The integration strategy of the second acquisition was intentionally designed in a different way. The executive team decided to run the acquisition as a stand-alone unit and avoid the risk of overwhelming the market with their merging efforts. Both companies kept their own processes, planning and inventory management systems, their own customer and technical service centres.

The first real synergy and optimization efforts only started six years later with an operational excellence programme. This standalone strategy seemed to create less obvious disturbances to the customers than the first M&A, but after a few years, the team concluded that, with the exception of some line extensions, their innovation pipeline was empty.

Going back to the due-diligence phase of this second acquisition, we clearly see that the acquiring organization assumed it had bought a robust innovation pipeline, but the market acceptance hadn't been tested, and the growth assumptions turned out to be totally off. Nobody had challenged those assumptions. We ask him whether not challenging assumptions and plans was a symptom in the company.

'Yes!' he almost shouts. 'It was, and we transferred that to our M&As.'

Which brings him to his third experience, the spin-off which is now one year ago and is so far considered successful.

'We got much better in challenging the assumptions in the pre-decision phase. We learned from the past and did some thorough introspection, including a cultural assessment to understand our own dynamics.'

When we explain to him the systemic principles and some of the potential restoring dynamics or entanglements, he gives this first phase a reasonably good score. The organization understood the need to form a new identity and define a clear purpose for the newly formed company that clearly distinguishes it from the past. In their eagerness to do so, he admits they were distancing themselves from the past identity rather than honouring the roots, but they had been pretty successful so far in establishing a new order in the executive team and below, and igniting passion and energy throughout the organization.

When we ask him to describe the critical success factors for M&As based on his experience, he lists:

- Look beyond your own organizational system when designing the integration. Expand it to include the value chain, and most importantly the customers. Keep them top of mind and in sight.

- Strong communication to the customers. Offer them clear and easy-to-follow transition guidelines. Keep the complexity in-house; don't put it on the customers.

- Leadership requires a healthy mix of home grown and fresh blood.

- Early clarity around decision making. Who has the authority?

- Understand and be honest about your own culture to better evaluate the cultural match or mismatch.

- Focus on the human element of the integration and clarify the opportunities in the new situation.

This involves extensive internal communication and training.

- Putting it all together is comparable to taking it apart. His experience of going through the two difficult M&As was tremendously helpful to work through the spin-off.

Questions for reflection

- What is the relevant system in the post-merger phase?

- Did you include the customer?

- What is the impact on your customers of your inorganic growth plans? How do they benefit from it?

- Do you fully understand your own culture?

- How do you assess cultural compatibility of a future partner or acquisition target?

4
The Systemic Principles

'Every system is perfectly designed to get the
results it gets.'
  —W Edwards Deming

Setting the stage

In our interactions with executive or change teams, we
often put this thought-provoking quote on the table as
an opening statement. We would like to see the concepts and learnings from our research that we share
in this book applied in a proactive way to set M&As
up for success before the ink is on paper, but as we are
typically not called in when everything is bright and
shining, this quote often gets push back at first.

The M&A deal is signed, the synergies between both parties have been identified, the savings carefully calculated, the new business processes redesigned by intelligent people. The integration plan was considered ambitious yet achievable, but still results are lagging or even declining. The newly formed company is trying to form a new system composed of two or more partners, each with its individual underlying dynamics.

The way we have experienced working with the **systemic principles** is that they support us to identify and understand the symptoms in companies and organizations, leading us to the underlying dynamics, and that they can be used as the compass to navigate through the never-ending complexity and change in volatile and unpredictable times. The four main systemic principles we use are the result of a multidisciplinary field of research and phenomenological experience, and can be seen as the natural laws of systems translated to the business reality. As we will illustrate with stories from our own experience, not respecting these principles creates entanglements or constrictions which lead to unhealthy dynamics and unintended consequences, often reflected in disappointing or disastrous results, loss of market share, a demotivated workforce, talent depletion, etc. Understanding and respecting these principles leads to flow, and the ultimate goal is to use them at all times to navigate in a dynamic, complex environment. In our experience, these principles are globally applicable with local specificities.

The systemic principles are:

- Purpose

- Connection and inclusion

- Order and occupying one's place

- Exchange

Let's examine the four principles in detail.

 Purpose

Most executive leadership teams believe that they have clearly defined their purpose, which they have described and nailed to the wall as a vision statement. Having seen many of these, we sometimes feel that these teams only have a limited vocabulary to tap into. With a small, exhaustive list of words to choose from, their only freedom lies in the construction of the sentence. The 'best' and 'highest' are often combined with terms like 'quality', 'safety', 'customer satisfaction', 'delivery excellence', 'innovation', 'sustainability' and 'employee satisfaction'. The organization is striving for zeros in areas like footprint, incidents, negative community impact and energy consumption while doubling revenue, market share, market penetration and net promoter score, preferably all to be achieved by a nicely rounded year in the future.

We mean something more than these vision, mission and strategy statements when we talk about purpose. In essence, it comes down to this key question: 'What is society inviting you to contribute to?' This might sound naïve at first, but in essence it defines purpose in connection with the world around you. This broader definition of purpose will be vital for the long-term sustainability of the company. What is the deeper need your company is asked to fulfil? Just 'beating competition', 'doubling market share' or 'penetrating another regional market' is not what we mean. As an authority in disruption and sustainability sharply stated in his key note to a top leaders team: 'Will the world be better off, if your company doubles in size?'

There are numerous examples of companies that have not been able to adjust their course the moment society ceased to value what they were doing, or when that need was suddenly met by a cheaper or higher value replacement product or service. They stayed attached to their isolated purpose for a long time, leading to a total decline or bankruptcy. Obviously, there are as many examples of companies that did understand their business model or strongest brand was reaching its shelf life and have been agile in finding a new purpose, but it's important they keep the true meaning of purpose in mind.

Systems strive to survive. We have seen many examples of compensating mechanisms covering up the early warning signals indicating that the company needed to repurpose in response to shifting societal and market dynamics. Companies directing all their attention and their most experienced resources to one large contract while losing sight of refilling the pipeline. Strategic planning teams suggesting one acquisition after the other, burdening the newly acquired partners with a mother company that lacks innovation.

When it's well understood and defined in relation to the broader societal needs, a strong purpose gives creative direction to an organization, confirms its right to be in the game and offers it valuable insights to stay agile in an ever-changing environment.

Next to purpose, we are also interested in a company's leading principles. Generally, they will be a subset of the purpose; companies often refer to their core values as their leading principles. We will always challenge whether they really are, because the framed list of core values on the wall sometimes looks more like a wish list than a purpose.

A clear leading principle will inspire each individual to do what they do daily, to persevere in times of adversity or run the extra mile to safeguard high standards or excel. But even within the same industry and company, the leading principles can vary for different parts of the organization. Dealing with the resultant conflicts, bottlenecks or pain points in the system is one of the key ongoing challenges in the larger set-up.

We found one of the most obvious examples in the healthcare industry. Even though this industry is built on the same foundations with a true purpose of taking care of the sick and disabled in society, the different professions within the medical crew of a hospital, mental institution or care home often have different leading principles. Doctors, physicians or surgeons, as they have confirmed by taking the Hippocratic Oath, are mostly focused on curing and repairing. As a result, they may be striving to keep their patients alive for as long as possible, initiating treatments accordingly. The nursing and care-taking crew members spend more time close to the patient and have quality of life as their number-one leading principle. Being aware of this innate conflict and finding the right balance is a crucial cross-functional challenge for the industry to operate as a unified system.

When a purpose and leading principles are cascaded down into the organization, it brings the decision power to the right level, allowing each echelon to focus on the right combination of run, maintain, innovate and regenerate. The key question in a M&A is whether the purpose of both parties is compatible or whether you can find a future common purpose that will lead the way for the newly formed family. With a few notorious M&A disasters in mind, we maintain that a superficial answer to this question is not sufficient. There is an additional question to add here: 'What is the purpose of the M&A itself?' There is obviously a strategic intent and ambition for it, but what lies behind the plans for inorganic growth, vertical or horizontal integration, doubling the market share or expanding to new industries or territories?

In all our interactions, whether it is in an interview during a diagnostics phase or in a strategy session with the C-suite or the integration team, we will ask the following question at a certain point in time: 'What is this merger or acquisition an excuse for?' That might sound like a strange question at first, but every single person we have asked to date has had an immediate answer to it. They may never have thought of the M&A as an excuse for something else until we asked, but then they could all pinpoint the exact thing that made it a diversional tactic. What fundamental issue was not addressed? Which critical quality was missing? What needed to stay hidden?

CASE STUDY: WHAT WAS THE POINT?

'Would you have approached it differently in hindsight?' is what we asked an executive team that was about to spin off a business unit they had acquired some eight years ago. They were communicating to the departing organization's employees that they would be better off on their own, that they would be able to take their future in their own hands now. Being a part of the big mothership was holding them back; the industry dynamics and cyclical economical turns of the two parties were fundamentally different.

If that was true, what was the purpose of the M&A in the first place?

Purpose, as defined and experienced in our systemic work, is the North Star for the organization. It is important to know that the true purpose and the leading principles will positively impact customers' and employees' day-to-day reality. When you understand that an M&A will always shake up or overhaul the direction you have set for your company in ways that you might not have foreseen, it is essential in the critical pre- and PMI phase to ask yourself a few purpose-related questions:

- Is the purpose still clear?

- What is society's request to you?

- Does the purpose need to be redefined?

- Will you be able to gather the combined employees of both organizations behind it? How?

- Is this acquisition masking something else?

Connection and inclusion

Everybody who belongs to the system is entitled to have their place

'The system prevails over the individuals,' is one of our more provoking statements; provoking because the common belief is that people are your organization's most valuable asset – literally your human capital – and they can influence the success of the business with their vision, decisions and actions. We believe that these two concepts are not contradictory. Value for the human factor, creating a workplace where there is flow and vitality, is what we are striving for, but who you need – how many people, which roles, what skillsets, etc – depends on your purpose. It's not a matter of creating space for all, to give everybody a sense of belonging and work; the task is to create the organization you need to achieve your goals.

The company's purpose and ambitions for the next period in relation to its environment will define the right organizational design, resulting in a certain structure with different departments, layers and roles to be filled. It's critical for each individual, and equally for each department or business unit or plant site, to know and understand their place in the system, which will define their contribution to the whole. With constructional issues or a lack of clarity, the foundation of the entire system is shaky. For example, adding a customer-care department without clarifying its role and redefining the role of the existing customer-service department impacts the entire organization. Internal planning and production won't understand who decides on priorities and who is authorized to intervene in the production wheel anymore.

How does everyone having their place in the system play out in an M&A?

CASE STUDY: MERGING LEGACIES

We worked with a merged banking cohort on some of their people processes. In the demographics part of their annual employee engagement survey, they offered the respondents two options: ex-company A and ex-company B, sometimes also referred to as legacy A and legacy B. In other words, people were being boxed into two groups, connected to the past.

On top of that, there was a third group of people who didn't know what to select as they had joined the company after the merger. They had no attachment to either of the original companies, but neither were they able to connect to the new identity as the rest of the organization was still living in the past.

Before we could connect everybody to the new name on their business cards, we decided to bring the layer of distinction to the surface. We physically made two areas A and B in the room and positioned the newcomers at the door. Then we asked the two groups to reconnect to their own past.

They reflected on the historical characteristics they wanted to bring into the future culture and on the elements they consciously wanted to leave behind. Each group shared their pride, their frustrations, their sense of loss, their critical competencies, while the other groups had the opportunity to ask questions, comment, suggest different ways of achieving the same and buy in to each other's wishes. Only then did we invite everybody back into the centre of the room.

When we use this principle of connection and inclusion for departments, functions and people, we see certain prevailing feelings and emotions like mourning, loss or exhaustion. It is vital to connect to whatever the team is asking for in terms of attention and inclusion so that the system can find its way back to health and flow.

Many different dynamics will occur when this principle is not respected, as illustrated in the next chapter.

Nobody can leave the system unnoticed

If you have ever seen Russell Crowe in Ridley Scott's *Robin Hood*, you might recall him in the guise of Sir Robin Longstride giving the death notice of King Richard Lionheart to the King's mother. When he hands over the crown to her, you see the pain on her face for just one moment, and then she crowns her younger son John by saying: 'The King is dead, long live the King.' The witnessing noble and peasant crowd instantly kneels down for the new King.

Even though we have watched this movie several times, this moment always leads to a kind of sad and awkward feeling that whoever we are, we will never be irreplaceable. We might even be immediately forgotten, our position refilled the moment we walk out and close the door behind us.

Interestingly enough, this is comparable to how many companies handle significant changes. We hear phrases like:

> 'You have been with this company for twenty-seven years. We have just been acquired by a large foreign investor. We have exciting times ahead of us. We value your loyalty to the new owner.'

> 'As a result of the synergy analysis, we have decided to let go of Peter and Suzanne. Today was their last day. We will eliminate some of their tasks and distribute the remaining work to the rest of the team. Apart from that, nothing else will change for you.'

Many organizations forget to say goodbye to people and to honour their contributions. They assume that the people who stay will go back to normal right away, denying the fact that there is a new and unknown 'normal' and the employees may have strong attachments to the old way of working, the well-known dynamics, the long-held relationships, the traditions and banter. As a result, the employees who stay feel their colleagues – often their friends – have left the system 'unnoticed'. Their attention and energy will still be focused on the empty spaces in the teams, prohibiting them from moving on and adjusting to the new reality.

We have seldom seen an M&A with zero departures, and most of them have a significant people impact. The synergy calculations often result in multi-layered spreadsheets demonstrating the efficiency and productivity per capita at the end of the restructuring, but the stretch targets are seldom reached as this would require the people who stay to be fully on board, motivated and dedicated.

Remember we are operating in Cynefin's area of complexity when executing the integration plans after a merger or acquisition. The perfect analysis is not a guarantee for success. As M&As usually include restructurings and retirement plans, consciously holding yourself to high standards when it comes to personnel departures and guiding the remaining workforce through the mourning phase is one of the critical interventions we advise on in almost every engagement.

 ## Order and occupying one's place

Where the previous two principles define what the newly formed company needs to reach its purpose – the organizational structure, which departments, how many people, which talents and skills – and acknowledges the fact that each department and individual is entitled to a place in the system, this principle expresses the need to understand the order, make it transparent and act accordingly. What is each person's place in the system? How can they fully occupy it?

We are living in times of self-managing shifts, virtual organizations, leaders who are visible on the shop floor and interacting with their teams on a daily basis, new organizations built on a small-base structure with mostly freelance connections, so you may wonder whether this concept of order is outdated. It is critical to understand that order does not only equal hierarchy; it might in some cultures or companies, but order can be based on many different aspects.

Every system has its intrinsic order. If everybody and every subsystem has its place in the whole, order will define what that place is exactly, and how each function contributes to the purpose, what is to be expected from each one and who comes first. Pretending that there is no order or not honouring the intrinsic order will lead to some interesting self-regulating dynamics, to say the least.

What defines the order of assets, business units, departments or functions, leaders and employees? There is really no single answer to this question.

CASE STUDY: DINOSAURS

Soon after the acquisition of a global Scandinavian company by an American player, we were hosting leadership forums for the C-level and the next layers of leadership. As we did the introduction roundtables, the leaders from the acquiring company introduced themselves by their names, their titles and their number of years' service with the company, which ranged from eighteen to thirty-five years. The higher the number, the prouder the employee.

In a smaller group session the next morning, the newly acquired leaders expressed that they were horrified by this length of service. In their innovation-driven environment, people were valued for bringing in new perspectives and experience from other industries and corporations, trying new ventures and failing fast. They felt they had landed in an antiquated and rigid environment with a bunch of grey-haired dinosaurs who had never set foot out of their company and their area of expertise.

The task for this combined set of leaders was not to argue over which culture was superior, but to acknowledge the differences.

Order among people can be determined by:

- Leading principle – what is leading? Curing and fixing, or quality of life? Being a production company, in which case the operational roles will be high in the order, or being a solutions provider where the production source is less relevant?

- Financial stake in the business – partners who have made a personal investment are higher in the order than associates who have not.

- Hierarchical position and breath of responsibility. Responsibility does not necessarily equal power or might, but rather the weight and width of the responsibility for a larger whole.

- Seniority in the company, in the role, or in a specific field of expertise.

- Title, role or pay level.

It can also be defined by:

- Nationality

- Educational level

- The rank/order defined by society (societal class, military rank, etc)

- Contribution to the business results

- Political preference or religion

There is no right or wrong answer, but it is important to understand what the order is based on. That allows you to question whether it is still beneficial to achieving your purpose and strategic vision, and to redefine it when needed.

In our experience, it is not necessary to redefine the order of a newly merged organization immediately, as it may be unclear in the beginning how to find common ground. Simply naming the differences removes a lot of uncertainty or frustration and invites the entire organization to co-create the new identity. The word 'dinosaur' became a part of the integration story in that company, which brought some humour to the teams in the hectic months after the acquisition. Only at a later stage on the integration path were they ready to reconnect to the new direction, the strategic growth path and purpose after acquisition, and decide from there what the criteria for leadership assignments and development needed to be going forward.

The same criteria can be used to understand the order in the executive leadership team. We once did an introduction on systemic intelligence with global executives who were leading a declining business. They were in charge of the only consulting business unit within a large production-oriented company.

To illustrate the importance of order, we asked them to:

- Line up in order of number of service years with the mother company

- Change the line-up based on the number of service years with the consulting business unit, which led to a totally different picture

We discussed with them which line-up was more relevant, given the fact that the nature of the business unit was fundamentally different from the typical product-based business. Some of the leaders had never worked for any of the other business units but had in-depth consulting experience. Others were proud of their long career with the mothership and were still figuring out how to translate that experience to a consulting and service environment.

The main insight came with our last instruction, which was to ask the executives to line up in order of contribution to the business. We were curious what would happen, and in this specific case it led to a total freeze. Nobody was moving. We could sense the discomfort this instruction had caused. Some were trying to make a joke out of it, others wanted to understand what the criteria were.

In a few minutes, we had an illustrative demonstration of the paralysis also present throughout the organization. In their identity shift to a full consulting company, with ever-changing directives and KPIs, the employees didn't know anymore how to contribute to the business performance. Two years later, after a spin-off where they became an independent consulting company, in partnership with an investor, the global leadership team grabbed the opportunity to fundamentally rethink purpose and order and align the global troops behind a clear common goal.

Defining the new board composition and assigning the most attractive positions is often part of the M&A negotiations. It is not uncommon to base this on status, power or equal distribution of board seats, but examining the order that is most favourable for the future of the company usually surpasses the negotiated composition of the newly appointed board.

Order is not only defined on an individual or leadership level; it also defines the priorities in the organizational structure and the relationships between departments.

CASE STUDY: 'WE ARE A MANUFACTURING COMPANY'

We were reflecting with a former COO on the large operational excellence journey he had embarked on during a major acquisition, impacting over 200 sites, of which 25% were newly acquired manufacturing plants. As we were asking him some systemic questions, we jointly realized that he had actually restored order with this endeavour.

One of his statements in every town-hall meeting, in every site visit, in every interaction with the chief executives was 'We are a manufacturing company.' By confirming over and over again that 90% of the company's products were manufactured in its own production facilities, he confirmed that manufacturing was the key value-adding process. The key leading principle, you could say. The company's science and intellectual property were not only hidden in the molecules, but in its competence to manufacture them on a large scale in a safe and cost-competitive way.

The new organizational design, installing a strong integrated operations function, and the global company-wide production system roll-out focused on repositioning, strengthening and improving all aspects of operations. It led to impressive performance improvements and a leading role for manufacturing going forward.

While this was a strategic and cyclical shift for the legacy sites, it was unprecedented for the acquired production facilities. All of a sudden, they found themselves getting:

- More respect
- More attention, follow-up and direct support
- Access to a regional and global network of subject matter experts and technology guardians
- Specific support from a continuous improvement facilitator and a mindset and behaviour coach

Except for a few site leaders who had created their own little kingdoms after many years of freedom to operate, employees of the acquired company perceived this as an upgrade – a step up in the order – which really got them motivated to embrace the changes. In the end it was a smooth integration with a fast adoption of the manufacturing and functional best practices.

We have seen the opposite in our work with one of the locations of a global player in a highly compliance-driven and regulated industry. As the previous owner of the site was driving local accountability and empowerment, the site leadership had achieved impressive results with its 'one factory' concept. Production was the value-adding process step, so the leaders had arranged the entire organization – the role of the support functions, the site layout, the KPIs and the daily routines – to assure that the manufacturing crews could achieve their goals. When it was acquired by a company with a more top-down approach and functions set up as global competency centres, the leadership team had to fight numerous battles to hold on to what they had achieved. They referred to this corporate functional invasion as 'functional extremism'.

This specific site had some authority to speak up and hold their ground, as they were the 'new release' site, where all new products were prototyped, tested and qualified, and therefore critically important within the asset network. This gave them a higher position in the rank, compared to other sites. Other plants that were mainly producing commodities would not have been able to hold on to their operating model; the strong top-down functional culture would have overruled them.

Business units or assets are also bound by a certain order. Criteria to define this order could be:

Size

The larger sites are often the ones with the authority, resources, competencies and capacity to pilot new products, processes, change programmes, etc. We often see a mentor approach, where the large facilities get the additional task to provide expert assistance and coaching support to one or more younger or smaller sites, often within the same country or business unit.

Contribution to revenue, profitability or cash flow

In most companies with an extended asset footprint, there is a large variety in the contribution of the different business units and sites. Some are the eternal cash cows, while others are in a constant struggle to survive. This unbalance can have many reasons: product portfolio, local labour cost, plant layout and age, etc. While it is important to make the order of assets transparent, it is our experience that an eternal unbalance in contribution to the business results will lead to disruptive dynamics (the next systemic principle of exchange).

Product portfolio

The specificity of the product portfolio can determine its importance within the overall network, whether it is new release, a specific demanding range of products, a sole supply product, the most important brand, the most important ingredient for other manufacturing sites, or a customer-critical stock-keeping unit. These specific attributes might lift the unit or site higher up in the ranks.

Nationality/history

Order can be overruled when nationality and history play an important role. This often not expressed openly, but when you ask people within the organization, everybody seems to know that the founding site remains 'untouchable' or that all locations in the headquarter country are less impacted by restructurings, even when their performance does not justify a different treatment.

Nationality and history sometimes seem to play a role in defining the order. Even when this is a conscious decision, maybe even a critical one in the founding and early growth years of a company, the moment the company aspires to be truly global, favouring the founding country over the others can lead to unhealthy dynamics and even pose a risk to the long-term sustainability. Bringing together two companies with strong patriotism without addressing attachment to the founding nationality often leads to an unspoken discord for years to come. We will illustrate in later chapters what can be done to debottleneck a situation like this.

There is no single approach to order. There is no one answer, no right or wrong. It is not static. After a merger or acquisition, significant restructuring, a change programme or strategic shift, or following changing market needs, the criteria for order will alter. Our main goal is to support you to navigate in times of change with order as one of your instruments.

Ask yourself:

- What is the official order within the organization, and what are the unwritten rules that are defining the real order?

- What are some of the restraining forces inhibiting the organization from achieving its purpose and performance targets?

- How can you make them transparent and engage the organization in redefining the right order?

This principle has a second element to it: once the order is clear, it is critical to make sure everyone is actually fully occupying the place that they have in the system – not the seat above, not the ones below, not someone else's seat – and taking the full responsibility that comes with it. Is everyone in alignment with the order that is needed to achieve the purpose? Is anyone constantly overstepping their own role and assuming someone else's area of responsibility? Is anyone leaving their seat vacant?

We have seen critical seats being left open, either by organizations not filling them or by the person occupying the seat being distracted by something else. We witness leaders with one foot in their middle managers' roles, micromanaging them to total disempowerment. We observe informal influencing and lobbying processes outside of the order. All of these manifestations of not respecting the principle of order and occupying one's place will lead to destabilizing dynamics that often outlive the people involved. In the next chapter, we will dive deeper into the entanglements related to all four principles.

The three principles we've discussed so far – purpose, connection and inclusion, and order and occupying one's place – and the relationship between them form the essential structure of an organization. They are the foundations and the building. This structure is the holding ground for the energy exchange that needs to happen to create flow and achieve success.

But how do we breathe life into this structure?

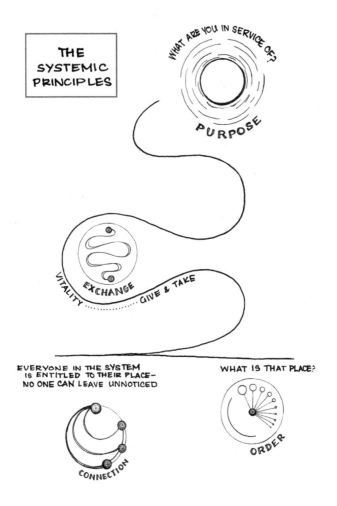

THE SYSTEMIC PRINCIPLES

WHAT ARE YOU IN SERVICE OF?

PURPOSE

VITALITY

EXCHANGE

GIVE & TAKE

EVERYONE IN THE SYSTEM IS ENTITLED TO THEIR PLACE – NO ONE CAN LEAVE UNNOTICED

CONNECTION

WHAT IS THAT PLACE?

ORDER

Exchange

We can design the perfect skeleton, structure it and define the interconnections between all parts, but how do we inject life into it? What does it take to create energy, flow and vitality; to assure that all these elements are interacting in an upward spiral? The company's founding idea created the initial spark, but it is not necessarily an Olympic flame.

Let's expand on this metaphor:

- Sunrays are reflected from mirrors to ignite the Olympic flame (the magic of the founding inspiration)

- In a relay, the Olympic torch is handed over from one runner to the next (energy flowing through the different generations of a company, from the founder to their successor, to the next CEO, and so on)

- Once, the Olympic flame was passed to divers, keeping the fire alive underwater (it is possible to keep the company spirit alive, even through strategic repositioning or unusual or rough times)

- The flame is only extinguished during the closing ceremony of the Olympic Games (when a company has fulfilled its purpose, the fire dies out, unless there is a new purpose on the horizon)

- If the Olympic flame dies along the way, it cannot simply be reignited with another torch; it needs the sun and the mirror once more (there is no easy fix when vitality is gone; it requires some real soul-searching to understand what caused the energy depletion and find out how to reconnect to the founding spark)

The systemic principle of exchange explores the mechanism of movement and energy flow by looking at the balance between giving and taking; between debit and credit; between what you owe the company and what it owes you in return. This balance needs to be looked at over a certain period of time; the organization will not be in full equilibrium at every given moment, but a lasting or stagnating unbalance will lead to unpredictable restoring dynamics that are energy depleting. While striving for balance, we will have to accept and work with unbalance.

In a company with a healthy exchange, you will see constant movement. It delivers products to its clients and gets paid in return. The founders or company owners are carrying the investment and the risk, so they are entitled to a part of the profit in return, as the employees they hire are not carrying the same burden. Employees sign a contract that grants them a salary and benefits in return for their skills, time and commitment, and they get paid only after they have delivered the work. You can ask people to run the extra mile during peak load moments or in times of crisis, but that needs to be compensated for in the form of:

- Financial compensation

- Recognition

- Learning and personal growth opportunities

- Promotion perspectives

- Being part of a high-performing team

- Other compensating mechanisms

Assets that are consistently contributing to the profitability more than others need to see the benefits. These assets, often called cash cows, could be first on the list to get assigned an expansion project, access to additional capital investment money, permission to invest in upskilling. But you may have heard the expression 'We have been milking the cow for too long.'

In view of an M&A, the concept of exchange gets a bit more complicated. The owners or board members sign off on a significant amount of money to acquire a company's name, brands, network of assets, client relationships, access to new territories and markets, and every individual who is contracted. They typically have a personal financial stake in the game and gain professional standing, respectability and an expanding track record of important deals.

But their pride and excitement might not always be shared by the organization. Even when the objective elements seem to predict good fortune, they are the ones who need to make it happen.

For the employees, the merger or acquisition can feel like a forced and hostile takeover. The contract signature at the highest level does not guarantee that employees will be excited and willing to exchange their experience, knowledge, skillsets, motivation and loyalty for compensation and new benefits. It's only at the highest levels that 'What is in it for me?' is closely related to 'What is in it for the whole system?' As employees feel they're being taken over, they experience a feeling of loss at first, so may not immediately be open to discovering what the new exchange could look like, and what additional opportunities for learning and growth there are in forming a new system.

Part of our intervention in the early phase of integration is to help people see the chances and possibilities to influence the new company identity while many things are still fluid. We also support them to express what they have lost that will not come back, at least not soon. Our experience leads us to conclude that there is only a limited window of time to get the new narrative right and engage the whole organization in it. Soon after day zero, the story gets crystallized in people's minds and hearts, and it then requires much more effort to rewrite it.

So far, we have reviewed the key characteristics of systemic intelligence and the critical competencies to navigate in complexity. We have walked you through the range of systemic principles – your navigation instruments along the way. In the next chapter, we will share some important dynamics and symptoms that you might interpret in a different way when looking at them through the systemic lens.

A True Story: The Pecking Order

'What is the new pecking order based on?' we ask him.

The meeting is not about the organization's history of acquisitions; it is about transformation and change management in the organization, but very early on in the discussion, our 'M&A alarm' goes off.

The man on the other side of the table has a long history of service in this company. He is close to retirement and doesn't have anything to prove anymore. In the last decade, he has led one of the major functions in the company, and recently he gave his open and honest opinion to the CEO about the cultural issues and the leadership gaps he was seeing. As a result, the CEO released him from his duty and gave him a new mandate: he is now leading the cultural change journey for the company. That's about it in terms of the mandate – no scope or boundaries; no team or budget; just limitless freedom. The board is fully supportive and has given him eighteen months to complete the change.

When he describes the organizational design to us, including roles and responsibilities, that's when we ask him about the M&A history. The current state is best described as a joint venture between two big players, both the result of a sequence of acquisitions before one was acquired by the other. One had a clear common identity with profit-and-loss accountability spread over different product-line businesses. The other – the buyer – was managed as a holding company with limited corporate guidance.

The newly composed board and executive team decided on a corporate top-down approach. They are convinced that all the best practices are to be found somewhere within the company; it's just a matter of discovering them and implementing them everywhere.

The reality in the field is somewhat different. Leveraging between all the sites is not supported at all by the systems. Regions and hubs are acting as local kingdoms. One region works in total isolation; the others are willing to share their knowledge and best practices but are not interested in receiving. The

behaviour that is currently rewarded is the hero attitude – the ones who are saving the day, no matter
how, are cheered.

When we ask him the pecking order question totally
out of the blue, he looks at us and smiles. He instantly
gets what we are asking. The previous CEO of the
merged entity was a charismatic leader, coming from
one of the legacy companies. The new CEO comes
from the other camp and is more of a hands-on char-
acter. The previous CEO was invited to come back
after a short break and is now the chairman of the
board. He has a close relationship with the chief financial officer (CFO). The rest of the executive team is a
mix of both parties.

While the executive dynamics keep the top leaders
busy, the message of corporate standardization and
leveraging is not cascaded down, or is simply ignored.
The regional and sub-regional leaders run their show;
it's what they know and what made them successful
in the past, but they are now losing market share at
an alarming speed. Sales effectiveness is declining,
the combined sales teams are not getting a clear direction and are not managed properly. Some segments
are faced with commoditization and are not ready
to adjust their operational cost structure and modus
operandi to the new environment.

The organization tried a large corporate performance
transformation a few years ago. It was not successful.

The recent pulse survey in the organization shows low morale.

We want to understand where he sees the company on the continuum scale, from being a holding structure to a complete integration under one identity.

'That's exactly the point,' he replies. 'We say that we want to be one strong identity, but nothing we do is congruent with that ambition.'

Questions for reflection

- Where do you want your organization to be on the continuum from a holding structure on one end to full integration on the other? What are the consequences?

- What is the new 'pecking order' based on?

- How is the new leader positioned and perceived by their executive team and the entire organization?

- What is the new model for decision making? Is it transparent?

- What KPIs are you measuring post-merger? What behaviours are you driving with these KPIs?

5
Entanglements And Dynamics

'You think that because you understand "one"
that you must therefore understand "two"
because one and one make two. But you forget
that you must also understand "and".'
—Donella H Meadows

Setting the stage

We defined the four systemic principles in the previous chapter:

- Purpose

- Connection and inclusion

- Order and occupying one's place

- Exchange

In reality, these principles are often connected and even reinforce each other. The dynamics – or entanglements – that we describe in this chapter will occur when one or more of the systemic principles are not respected. We could fill a complete book describing these entanglements or dynamics, and the multitude of symptoms with which they reveal themselves, so here we aim to name the most important ones connected to each of the systemic principles, or a combination of them, as this will give you plenty of diagnostic insights and interventions ideas.

OPERATIONAL DEFINITION: ENTANGLEMENTS

Our operational definition of entanglements in a business context is two or more elements (these could be people, departments, events, projects, decisions, etc) that have become bound to each other – mostly invisibly or unconsciously – in a way that reduces or eliminates the freedom to operate of one or all of the elements.

The table below names the entanglements as they are universally recognizable in organizational constellation and systemic works. For ease of explanation, we have categorized them according to the four principles and put them in the column where they mostly belong. As we are dealing with complex systems with multiple interdependencies, a specific dynamic will have elements of more than one principle in reality.

ENTANGLEMENTS/DYNAMICS (resulting from not respecting the systemic principles)

PURPOSE	CONNECTION and INCLUSION	ORDER and OCCUPYING ONE'S PLACE	EXCHANGE
Confusion	Exclusion	Leaving one's place to step into another one	Taking on someone else's burden
Hard work and no progress	Fighting someone else's battles	Powerlessness	Feeling deprived
Loss of meaning	Secrets	Triangulation	Honour/not honour
Paralysis	Extreme loyalty or no loyalty	Not taking one's place or responsibility	Blind obedience
No innovation	Too strong identification	Informal process influencing the formal one	Silent sabotage
	Projection		Neglect
	Disconnect		

 ## Entanglements/dynamics related to purpose

Examples of dynamics when the systemic principle of purpose is not respected:

- The organization is confused. The purpose is unclear, constantly changing or not connected to the needs of the outside world. People are doing what they think is best.

103

- Pressure is increasing as the critical numbers are not achieved. People are asked to work harder, fight fiercely for market share, reduce spending, etc. Despite the extra efforts, revenue and profitability deteriorate even further. As one employee put it: 'The train is gaining speed, but it is not moving forward.'

- Employee engagement survey results show low motivation. A large percentage of the organization's employees indicate that they are considering leaving. People seem to have lost trust, but in reality, they can no longer identify with the company's purpose (vision and values).

- There is a decision vacuum. Everybody is waiting for the CEO and their top leaders to set the new direction. People are sitting back until the new rules of the game are clear. Even robust existing processes are not continued with the same discipline.

- The company is too slow to react to changing market conditions. It keeps optimizing its existing business model, products, go-to-market approach, etc and loses sight of the fact that the societal needs and wants have changed. There is a lack of innovative products and ideas.

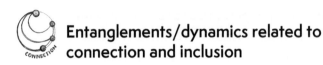

Entanglements/dynamics related to connection and inclusion

Examples of dynamics and symptoms when the systemic principle of connection and inclusion is not respected:

- The same department or leader gets excluded time and time again from the critical decision-making meetings. This could result in disconnected projects and initiatives, the activation of an informal information sharing and influencing circuit, silent sabotage, etc.

- Business or functional leaders get entangled in issues that don't impact them. Sometimes, they are even fighting for people who have already left. The organization is divided into two camps.

- A select group of people is aware of a secret in the organization. Discussions are held behind closed doors. Teams pick up the secrecy atmosphere and rumours start spreading.

- A big variation in loyalty. People with blind loyalty follow every order. Others have no loyalty at all.

- Total identification with the company's identity, making some leaders blind to objective analysis and facts.

- Projection – people appear to be overreacting. Emotions and resistance are much stronger than expected around a certain topic. In reality, they are projecting the feelings and emotions, the frustration and the hurt from a previous experience on to this one. Their old pain has been triggered.

- Disconnect between what the system needs on a deeper level and what has been created: non-existent places, employees not leaving a previous spot, interference between places because an employee's connection to it or loyalty to something/someone else is too strong. We would be triggered to explore this dynamic when we see a disconnect between the formal organizational chart and how the business is run in reality.

This last one deserves a few more words as it manifests itself in many different forms. Not creating clarity about the available places and who belongs where, or not intervening in case of drift, might lead to:

- More workplaces than the organization really needs. Everybody will keep themselves busy doing non-value-adding work or overlapping assignments.

- Special assignments for people to avoid making tough decisions. Even when the special assignment was value adding at first because of the specific skillset of one individual, often these places remain filled even years after that person has left the organization.

- Places that are critical for success left empty. Other people will tend to fill them.

- Two captains on one ship, both trying to assert themselves.

- The founder stepping aside, but remaining present as a board member so the new CEO can't take full accountability.

- A place is 'contaminated' or in a way still occupied because of the way the previous person left it (an abrupt departure following an ethics violation, the sudden death of a CEO, the previous CEO/owner still occupying an office next door, etc).

 Entanglements/dynamics related to order and occupying one's place

Examples of dynamics and symptoms when the systemic principle of order and occupying one's place is not respected:

- Indecisive leaders leaving their number one spot open by not setting the strategic direction or making tough decisions. This can lead to competing dynamics in the executive leadership team to influence the decision making. What they are actually trying to do is step into the shoes of the indecisive leader and fill the space that is left empty.

- First-line supervisors feeling powerless. The operations manager or functional leaders are micromanaging and stepping on the toes of the frontline leaders.

- Triangulation – people are being pulled into dynamics, into a conflict, into an open space between two leaders further up the hierarchy. Individuals are mediating at a level above them. This burdens them with a responsibility they can't manage.

- Decisions are not taken in the formal management reviews, but in unofficial meetings behind closed doors. The dynamics of the power play are unclear. Unwritten rules describe the way to get promoted to the top.

 ## Entanglements/dynamics related to exchange

Examples of dynamics and symptoms when the systemic principle of exchange is not respected:

- People are volunteering to do the work of others.

- The same hardworking individuals get burdened with every additional task or special assignment.

Then everyone is surprised when they leave unexpectedly or burn out.

- Certain teams feel that they are constantly denied recognition, compensation or a voice at the table.

- Individuals or teams feel that certain responsibilities or tasks have been taken away from them. They experience it as unjust and unfair, and silently sabotage the ones who took the tasks over.

- There is respect for certain values or traits, and not for others. People belong to the core group or they don't.

- Some individuals fanatically defend every leadership decision, without applying any judgement or common sense.

- Resistance is not openly expressed, but team members are silently sabotaging every new change initiative. They believe experience proves them right – it has never worked before and it will not work this time.

- A certain set of clients, a specific country or subsidiary, a team or a group of individuals are systematically neglected when the organization is deciding on a new approach. For example, new procedures don't take into account the reality in the smaller sites or remote locations. They don't account for the virtual teams, or for the legislation in a specific country.

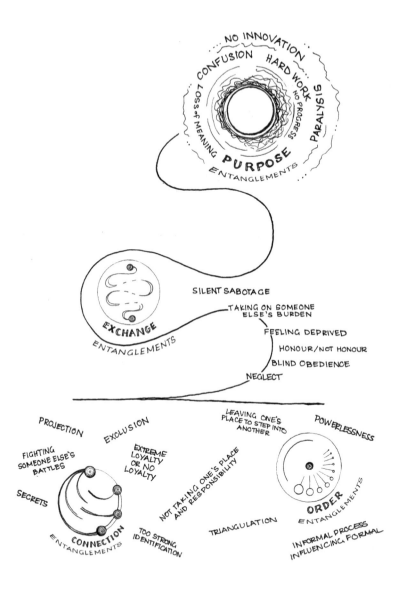

The above examples illustrate the symptoms and underlying entanglements you may see in one company or one part of the organization. As you can imagine, bringing together two parties after a merger or acquisition will not automatically resolve these issues. The dynamics will not be dissolved by designing a new logo, fixing a new nameplate on the door or printing new business cards, or by aligning the business processes and integrating the IT systems. On the contrary, you may be faced with unrecognized dynamics from both parties and additional symptoms as a result of a well-intended integration effort that totally misses the mark when you look at it from a systemic point of view.

In the next chapter, we will look at a different approach to M&As using systemic intelligence – one where we identify the most critical dynamics and symptoms, intervene, experience how the system reacts, and then decide on the next move.

A True Story: History Repeats Itself

While kicking off a trajectory with an executive team, we picked up from them the following history, originating in the 1970s.

Once upon a time, there was a young and ambitious chemical engineer. As this engineer had been able to stabilize a small manufacturing company a few years earlier and prevent it from falling into governmental hands, the founder decided to hand all his shares to this promising young man instead of his own sons.

After a fierce juridical battle that the sons lost, this young engineer, now the newly assigned owner, took over control of the organization and spent the next fifty years of his life building an empire spanning many different industries beyond manufacturing. The organization became active in retail, distribution, real estate, telecommunications and other segments, and the engineer became wealthy and famous in his own country. Working for this impressive holding came with a certain status.

During his lengthy and rich professional life, his heart was mostly in the original operational part of the company. He kept injecting money into manufacturing sites that were underperforming year after year in terms of profitability and productivity. Even in times of overcapacity, he would not take the tough decision to consolidate capacity and close some of the original sites.

As his retirement day was approaching, the owner finally surrendered to the idea of stepping back, but not without inventing a concept called the Co-CEO approach. He assigned two CEOs instead of one and kept an office next door.

The organization was led in parallel processes. The management team had executive committee meetings with and without the owner, leaving it unclear who was on the formal and the informal decision-making body. The entire organization was watching the arena fight between the two new CEOs. And just like in the movie *The Hunger Games*, there could only be one survivor. The defeated CEO finally left the company.

When we reviewed the organization's acquisition history and strategy, we found out that it was mostly based on buying local players that were not creditworthy, giving them little or no authority or opportunity to speak up. During the interviews, one of the executive committee members expressed his surprise that the organization had never been able to capture the knowledge it was trying to buy, nor optimize assets that were often in better shape than its own, nor hold on to strong leaders, experts and operators.

The biggest acquisition it had made was done ten years ago in a country up north. The initial holding set-up was managed via regional COOs with their own profit-and-loss accountability. But in a recent organizational redesign effort, the executive committee decided on a more central and functional structure and installed one COO with all plant managers reporting to him. That COO came in through the acquisition and, even though he had been a recent hire, he felt a strong attachment to the pre-merger company.

As he assigned a newly hired operational director, located in the south, in an intermediary role between himself and all the plant managers, the reality showed a two-camp picture. The plants in the north were bypassing the operational director and interacting directly with the COO. Their counterparts in the south did exactly the opposite.

As we kicked off the coaching journey with the members of the executive committee, they reported serious issues in some of the plants: trailing results in productivity, safety and quality; a high variability in the competencies of their local leaders and supervisors; a culture of complacency and 'creative problem solving' – in other words, people were taking shortcuts; and some recent catastrophic events.

As we retold them the story as we heard it, it dawned on them that this initial battle fifty years ago, was repeated over and over again at different times and at different levels of the organization

Questions for reflection

- Where in your company's history do you notice repeating patterns?

- When was the very first manifestation of that dynamic? What happened?

- Who was the last person (CEO, leader, expert) who was considered successful in that role?

- When you see dynamics related to all systemic principles, which intervention would give you the biggest lever? Which principle jumps out most strongly?

6
A Different Approach To M&A And Post-Merger Integration

'Does the walker choose the path, or the path the walker?'
— Garth Nix, *Sabriel*

Setting the stage

Are you willing?

Are you willing and able to reconsider your strategic intent and plans for inorganic growth? To look at the synergy calculations and integration plans through a systemic lens? To open up to the possibility that you might have created the very issues you need to fix now? To let go of what you know – allowing 'not knowing' to become part of your skillset – and experience what might happen if you intervene on a deeper level?

Personally, we have been amazed and excited to see how relatively small interventions can have a huge impact. How setting things right, according to these principles, creates relief, rest, flow, energy, vitality and joy in individuals, teams and companies and has an immediate visible impact on results.

There are many variables that will define our approach in a specific situation. In this chapter, we will describe the overall structure of diagnostics, envisioning and intervention.

Our diagnostics phase is often scheduled at the very beginning of the journey, but for us, it's a never-ending discovery as systems and their layers are constantly in motion. This is why navigation instruments are not only designed to plan for the voyage, but also to correct course along the way.

In the envisioning stage, we touch on the continuum with a holding structure on one end and a fully integrated identity on the other end, and many hybrid models in between. We will explore the consequences of the company's positioning – what it wants to be – along this line.

When leading interventions with a corporate team or on an individual level, we are tapping into many different fields of practice, including constellations, systems thinking, somatics, the theory of trauma in organizations, adaptive leadership, etc.[10] For ease of understanding, we will categorize the interventions based on the desired outcome or the movement we want to initiate. Most of all, we want to hand to you – managers, integration leaders, CEOs, COOs, HR directors, senior managers, group facilitators or change champions – an additional lens and skillset that is immediately applicable.

Diagnostics

Our diagnostics approach is never exactly the same as it depends on when we get involved in the PMI and what our mandate is. But we always want to find the deeper answers to the following three questions:

- Who are you/who were you (the life story of both parties in the M&A)?

- What are the symptoms at this moment?

- What are the underlying dynamics that create them? What are the forces at play?

Just as a global positioning system (GPS) uses different satellites to define exactly where you are now, where to find your destination, what the shortest, fastest or cheapest way is to get there and which roadblocks you will encounter along the way, we identify different sources of information and interactions from several angles to form our systemic view:

- Analysis of performance data

- Interviews and focus groups

- Workplace visits (headquarters, regional offices, production sites, distribution facilities, sales satellites)

- Constellation techniques

Who are you?

We will always want to know the life story of the initiating company. Whether we are invited in at an early stage when the strategic planning team is still scouting the market for interesting candidates, or in the due-diligence phase to complete the full scan of the new organization and potentially influence the bid price. Whether we are involved in the early integration phase when the new organization only exists on paper and the system is still in the 'chrysalis' process, or after things have got out of control and performance is lagging.

When the 'no-contact' period is over, and usually covered by a non-disclosure agreement, we would also want to dive into the archives and verbal traditions of the courted party as early as possible. Most often, the deal closure is long behind us, but it is still important to bring the history of the acquired company to life by interviewing the people who lived it.

- What is the company's identity?

- What is its history and heritage? How have these shaped its identity?

- How does it perceive itself?

- Who was (or were) the founder(s)?

- What was the first idea, the initial purpose, the founding spirit, the leading principle?

- Who funded the company in the early days?

- Which leaders shaped it? Which strategic decisions led it to growth and which left deep scars?

- What major historical or societal events have influenced its market position, reputation, cycles of growth and survival?

We typically draw the heritage timeline on the wall or tape it to the floor and mark all the milestones that were critical for the company's history, identity shifts and identity crises. These are not only the typical business events; we've had sessions with executive leaders where they've realized that the history of the company is closely connected to the triumphs and tragedies of the home country, or that the drastic decrease in employee engagement as demonstrated in the yearly survey started with the death of the long-retired founder five years ago. We mark the days that the company's 'crown jewels' were sold, when an explosion led to the death of three co-workers or when a fraud scandal was heading the news. Occasionally we name the role that some companies played in the World Wars.

Beyond knowing and naming these events, we mostly want to understand and feel their impact. Traumatic events in a company are stored in the visible and invisible structure, in its tissue and its collective memory. They still show in the internal relations and culture.

CASE STUDY: WALKING THE TIMELINE

We recently walked the company timeline with the fifteen executives of a major player in retail, projecting them back in time to the founding signature in 1821. We literally walked past all the critical moments in the company's history, the events and decisions that had shaped and shifted the identity and purpose to what it is now. Then we looked ahead into the future to the strategic shift ahead of it.

At the end of that activity, the CEO – who had joined the company only six months earlier and was under huge pressure from the shareholders, the market and the internal organization – spoke the following words:

'This past hour – reconnecting to the roots, remembering the influencers who have shaped this company over almost two centuries, understanding the decisions that got us here, hearing the stories of the ones who came in through an acquisition, seeing clearly what is still present from the past – felt like a real detox for me and my team.'

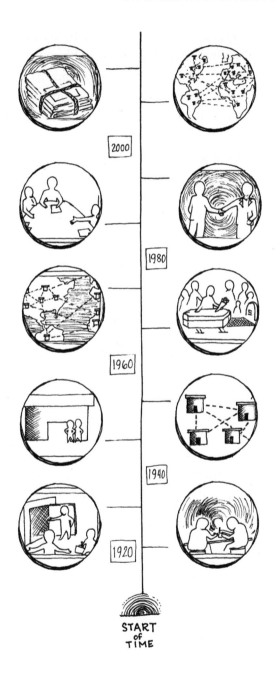

2000

1980

1960

1940

1920

START
of
TIME

After a merger or acquisition, we actually bring both parties' timelines into the room. Although the pre-merger history of the acquired party tends to be erased on the day of signature, its heritage remains in the hearts and minds of its people. It still resides in the assets that the acquiring company has bought or in the company structure and organizational tissue it has inherited.

When we are working with the timeline of compa-nies, we also look at generations. In our experience, the critical entanglements or the causes of some of the persistent struggles are regularly found a few genera-tions back.

In family systems it is obviously much easier to map the different generations. The family tree or geno-gram will separate the great-grandparents from the grandparents and on it goes, although children born to parents later in life or second families might create an overlap in time.

In companies, a transfer to a new generation is never black and white. It can be marked by different events: a transfer from the founding father to his children; a strategic shift in the company's purpose; the departure or retirement of a notorious or famous CEO; a major acquisition; an impactful economic crisis; expanding into another country or region. The length of a genera-tion can vary in time, and in these volatile times, we have observed a clear acceleration in turnover. In the past, there were longer periods of stability where 'this is how we work here' didn't fundamentally change; where teams were working as well-oiled machines and newcomers were adopted into the existing system. Is it too strong to say that those days are over?

A helpful thing to find out when working with a team is whether each relevant event, experience or story has a clear before and after date.

What are the forces at play?

There is a fascinating TED talk by ecologist Eric Berlow, who studies the interconnectedness of species, where he speaks about complexity in nature.[11] It perfectly illustrates how we can perform our diagnostics and map the system and the influencing forces.

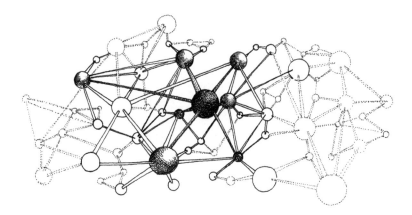

In fewer than five minutes, he makes several important statements that we can directly relate to our diagnostics approach in companies.

Complex ecosystems (statements from Eric Berlow)	Systemic intelligence in organizations	Our methodology/approach
The power of good visualization tools, which help you see patterns otherwise invisible to the human brain.	At a certain moment, stop talking: create a multidimensional picture and use other senses.	Diagnostics report that is mapping the system, the elements and its interconnections, instead of a root cause analysis of the problem.
		Mapping the force field: the restraining forces and the driving forces related to the problem.
		Constellation.
Ask questions you didn't think of before (previously invisible patterns revealed by the data help suggest questions you didn't consider).	Asking and listening for the systemic principles.	Systemic questions (covered later in this book).
	Core language: some words or statements have a different colour, sound, weight, or feel out of place.	Listen for core language.
		Listen to what is actually being said.

Continued

Complex ecosystems (statements from Eric Berlow)	Systemic intelligence in organizations	Our methodology/approach
Predictability: if you want to predict the effect of one species on another and you only look at that link (without considering the interconnectedness of the entire system), you will be far less likely to succeed.	We are often fighting the symptoms instead of solving the underlying dynamics. The solutions to these symptoms are typically making the situation worse.	Distinguish between the symptoms and dynamics, ie the entanglements (the underlying violations of the systemic principles). Look at the larger or whole system, not only at the distinct elements.
The larger the step back you take to look at the entire system, the more easily you will be able to identify the sphere of influence that matters most.	From the complex mix of systems overlaid on top of each other, what is the relevant system for the issue you are trying to solve?	Identify the relevant system. Intervene/experience/adjust.
The more you take in the entire system, the more you will find the easy answers.	A small intervention on a systemic level can have a big impact on the entire system.	Balcony/dance (be able to observe the whole and the dynamics, at the same time as being a part of them). Small interventions. Take the first step, experience and learn before taking the next first step.

Continued

Complex ecosystems (statements from Eric Berlow)	Systemic intelligence in organizations	Our methodology/approach
The easy answers are typically not the ones you considered before.	Be willing to let go of what you know and what you've learned. Working with the system can bring up a totally different answer.	Trust the wisdom of the system.
The answer is often no more than two or three degrees away from the initial 'knot' in the system.	The answer to the question is often no more than two or three generations back (two or three lines up or two or three lines out).	Broaden your scope in time and space. Start with the small things (interventions on a systemic level are not necessarily massive – it is all about finding the right acupuncture point).

Continued

Complex ecosystems (statements from Eric Berlow)	Systemic intelligence in organizations	Our methodology/approach
Some factors are actionable, others are not.	It is still possible to reduce the energy around events from the past by including and honouring their contribution. A change in one element from the system will automatically have an impact on the other elements. Some elements are unchangeable (at this moment), but most can be influenced.	Interventions that are focused on honouring the past and including traumatic events, so that the people in the system can open up to the possibility of a new future are hard.

We use different representation techniques to map the system and its spheres of influence and present it to the decision makers in a way that allows them to see the system.

- Listing the driving and restraining forces (also referred to as Kurt Lewin's Force Field Analysis)

- Overview of the different dynamics relating to the systemic principles

- A visual display (on the wall or floor) depicting the timelines of both parties, with the key milestones that have been defining for the identities of each one, sometimes adding important events from spheres of influence such as the home country, the industry, the holding company, the founding family, etc

- A constellation or *tableau vivant* of the team or situation to let participants see and experience the relations and connections within the system, or to fill in the missing links

- A metaphor to describe the systemic dynamics in an evocative way

- Techniques where we ask the participants to physically sculpt the current dynamic

- Multiple combinations of some or all of the above in different interventions

CASE STUDY: DIAGNOSIS

If your organization was a patient, what would your diagnosis be?

We were called in to diagnose the culture at one site as a pilot for an organization's larger asset network. We used systemic statements to introduce our four main themes, supported by evidence in terms of behaviour and processes, the visible impact and quotes from all the interviews we conducted within the organization.

Here is a brief summary of what we noticed:

Systemic perspective: the 'fixing' way out of problems often leads you back in.

Reality: what mindset and behaviour is the company really driving with its current approach and KPIs?

The site was under huge production pressure: its capacity was sold out, the overall equipment effectiveness (OEE)/uptime numbers on most lines were below 20%. Where the goal of the renewed leadership was to engage the organization in bottom-up improvement and create a problem-solving culture, what they were actually doing was pulling up the operational management at least two levels. The site director was focused on KPIs and action plans that belonged to the middle managers or even first-line supervisors.

Interestingly enough, we saw the same dynamic at the global level, resulting in a disengaged and disempowered crew, teams operating in silos, departments blaming each other for deviations, and despite all the efforts and pressure, no significant successes.

Systemic perspective: companies/sites with a strong DNA often have an equally strong immune system.

Reality: high pace of change and lack of transparency had led to lack of trust and resistance to change.

A widely-shared opinion at the organization's headquarters was that the site was resistant to change, hence we were called in. The site employees were of the opinion that they were going through constant change. They had a new site director who'd put together a 90% new leadership team, several headhunted from his previous company. The operations managers below the site leaders had been replaced, and half of the first-line supervisors were new to their role. Departments had been combined into one, others had been split or reshuffled, and a brand-new service had been established.

We used a metaphor to describe what we saw: 'For the employees in the site, many of them with a tenure of more than twenty-five years, this feels like being a patient recovering from a whole range of operations. You have transplanted two new lungs, given them stents, replaced their hips, put metal pins in one of the knees and laser treated both eyes. You've maybe even added a facelift along the way, and the patient's body is still considering whether to accept or reject all those new organs.'

Then the vice president of HR showed they'd understood by adding, 'And we are asking this patient to run a marathon.'

Systemic perspective: just like family systems, organizational systems have roots, history, memory and are still living the impact of previous generations.

Reality: people's energy is connected to the past. New hires are impacted by the low morale, and as such are included in the feeling of loyalty to the past.

From the initial conversations with people outside the site, we got some hints related to 'the old' and 'the new'. The veterans who had been there forever were viewed as resistant to change; the new people were the ones who wanted to move forward and were held back by the rest of the crew.

But we witnessed a different dynamic. Yes, people's energy was still going to the past. Everybody spoke highly of a site director from long ago, whose name and reputation as the father and protector of the organization was held high. He was the one who'd shielded them from the tedious headquarters. He was the one who'd assured highly competitive compensation and all kinds of benefits for his employees.

The interesting thing was that most of the new employees quickly adopted that story and the attachment to a past that they had never known. They were clearly welcomed and included, but the price they paid was to join in with the low morale.

Systemic perspective: the vitality in an organization is defined by the longer-term equilibrium between giving and taking.

Reality: people feel that a lot has been taken away from them and it is unclear what they will receive in return.

Digging into the historical context of the current work conditions, we understood two driving forces had influenced the positioning, HR decisions and industrial union relations:

- Determination and pride from the revered site director. More than one person quoted him as saying, 'No way would I ever want to call the headquarters to report a strike at the gate.' This attitude had led to amicable relations between the unions and the employer and a lot of 'cash for change' transactions, where every additional demand on the organization had to be financially compensated for by the company.

- His strong local network and presence, and his desire to make the site one of the most attractive employers in the area. As a result, the current site leadership team was faced with a set of compensation and benefit rules that were clearly outdated, given the current economic reality.

We are in no way intending to judge or blame that site director – he had been vital for the site's growth and right to operate – but it is extremely helpful to understand how the roots of current problems can date back a few generations. With the fast-paced changing of the guards over the last two years, well-intended leaders were trying to get out of the firefighting mode, but people only felt a sense of loss without any clarity about what was in it for them in the future.

Envisioning

Who do you want to be? Or rather, who do you need to be?

There is a line that we draw on the wall at the end of our diagnostics review with integration teams or leaders.

Who do you want to be as a company? Who do you want to become?

- Do you want to act as a holding company, where the different business units, regions, assets only share a name and the overall aspirations of the shareholders?

- Will you be a fully integrated organization with one new identity?

- Is your current optimum a hybrid model merging the best of both approaches?

There is no ultimate right or wrong answer, but this decision will have consequences. Not only on the organizational design, the tactical implementation plan, the KPIs and the performance management processes, it will also determine the requirements of the new system you are creating and the next steps that need to be taken. In essence, our leading question doesn't cover everything. It is not who you want to be, it's what you *need* the organization to be, given your purpose and strategic intent, and what is possible when building on the foundations of the past.

As simple as this may seem, we mostly see companies formally or informally deciding on one approach, and then behaving contradictorily to it. The narratives in town-hall meetings and press releases might talk about a merger of equals; a fully integrated company built on the strengths of two market leaders, each in its own field of expertise; a corporate sharing of best practices and a one-company approach, but in reality the sites or countries have full decision power, the functional dotted lines in the matrix organigram have no authority whatsoever and leaders run their own shows without consequences. Then the organizational design becomes dysfunctional.

The actual power play might jeopardize the synergy commitments following the merger, so day-to-day reality needs to match strategy. All the underlying confusions between the outer story and the inner truth, between the words on paper and the actual practices, will create entanglements in the system, some visible, many invisible, with negative effects.

The sweet spot on the continuum is not a static one. Strategic shifts will demand the leadership team to redefine who they need to be. Moving from a local to a global footprint, acquiring a company with strategic presence in uncharted territory, fundamentally different operational profiles, labour costs for shared services in different countries... all these elements will influence that leadership decision.

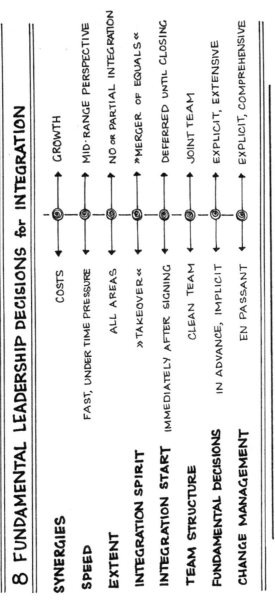

8 FUNDAMENTAL LEADERSHIP DECISIONS for INTEGRATION

SYNERGIES	COSTS	GROWTH
SPEED	FAST, UNDER TIME PRESSURE	MID-RANGE PERSPECTIVE
EXTENT	ALL AREAS	NO or PARTIAL INTEGRATION
INTEGRATION SPIRIT	»TAKEOVER«	»MERGER OF EQUALS«
INTEGRATION START	IMMEDIATELY AFTER SIGNING	DEFERRED UNTIL CLOSING
TEAM STRUCTURE	CLEAN TEAM	JOINT TEAM
FUNDAMENTAL DECISIONS	IN ADVANCE, IMPLICIT	EXPLICIT, EXTENSIVE
CHANGE MANAGEMENT	EN PASSANT	EXPLICIT, COMPREHENSIVE

POST-MERGER INTEGRATIONS — OLIVER WYMAN

Oliver Wyman identifies eight fundamental leadership decisions that must be explicitly made before the start of the integration to ensure a tailor-made, successful PMI process.

In those sliding-scale discussions with the strategy team or the integration task force, we want to assure that the conversation is happening on the systemic level and is not a theoretical or philosophical debate, but a guiding document for all next integration steps. It is not enough just to decide whether you want to task a clean team, with participants from only the acquiring partner, or a joint team. Not clarifying the structure that the leaders of both parties have agreed and the order it is based upon will tempt the whole system to restore order, leading to one or more of the dynamics we described earlier.

Systemic interventions

Throughout the book so far, we have mentioned constellations as one of the diagnostics and intervention techniques that we use. What do we actually mean when we say 'constellations'?

Yes, a constellation is a group of stars that forms outlines or meaningful patterns on the celestial sphere. That is not what we are referring to here, although the term 'meaningful patterns' is relevant. The use of constellation techniques originates in a combination of psychotherapy, somatics and systemic work. Its decades of application in family systems has been extended into organizational and societal systems.

OPERATIONAL DEFINITION: CONSTELLATION

A constellation is a representation of a system or part of a system that shows the relationships and influencing spheres. In our experience, you can illustrate it on a drawing board or flip chart, with objects on the table, or express it in a three-dimensional format in a *tableau vivant* using people and objects to represent parts of the entire system, key stakeholders or individual players.

Essentially, a constellation is a spatial representation of the elements and interconnections of a system. We often introduce it by saying, 'Let's bring the picture of the situation that is currently in your head out here in the room.' By doing so, we ensure the underlying dynamics and forces in the system become clearly visible.

The most important outcome of all systemic interventions is to restore the flow in the system and release the energy that is cut off or stuck somewhere. To clarify those words, picture a team or an organization that is 'in flow'. What would you see?

- Achievement of the targets, improving profitability

- Growth (in revenue, reputation, market leadership and impact)

- Innovative ideas

- Clients considering the company as their preferred supplier

- High morale – people are happy

- Easy collaboration and team work

- People dealing with differences in a constructive and proactive way

- Processes are running smoothly; problem solving happens quickly and is cross-functional

- Two-way and effective communication

We distinguish between two major processes that can seem like opposites at first sight, but in reality, they are more like communicating vessels flowing into each other. Doing one will create space for the other.

- Disentangle what is entangled

- Connect or reconnect what is disconnected

In other words, you unlock what is bound too tightly and attach what is loose or not connected.

Here are some examples of interventions related to these two streams:

Disentangle	Connect
Honouring the loyalty to the previous company so that people can let go...	... and create the space for connecting to the new reality/the new identity.
Honouring the contribution of a previous CEO to confirm their departure and farewell...	... so that the number one seat is empty again and can be fully occupied by the new CEO.
Remembering a tragic event that happened in the company (setting it free from its exile, not trying to negate it anymore)...	... so that there is room for mourning (connection to the loss) and the event becomes an integral part of the history (not silenced to death) to help the organization move on.
Understanding the founding spirit and heritage of the acquired party, including the conditions that led to it being taken over...	... so that its underlying or remaining strengths and qualities – including its people and assets – can be included and built upon.
In a spin-off – even though the spin-off organization is often relieved by the situation – honouring its roots and thanking the parent company for all opportunities provided	... so that the spin-off can seize the opportunity and form its own identity.

There is one constant in everything that we do:

Naming what is

- What has to be named?

- What are the facts? The dates, the numbers, the events?

- What needs to be spoken?

- What are you afraid to acknowledge, even though it is obvious?

- How can you name conflicting observations and accept that both can be true?

This is a lifelong journey for us, and no doubt for many people, as it requires courage, practice and an attitude of non-judgement. Yet speaking the truth and talking openly about what everybody observes or senses anyway is liberating. As the teams we are working with are often operating at high speed, we are the ones enabling them to pause, creating the time and the space to let these statements land and sink in. No fooling, no politically correct answers, no illusions. We often hear some deep sighs as the elephants in the room become visible, and as a result smaller and less threatening. A lot of the potential energy in a team or organization is wasted in hiding or suppressing the truth. It's like trying to keep a beach ball under water for a while; it costs a lot of effort, and the moment your attention wanders, it pops up again, smashing into your face.

Naming things is not the same as putting a strong point of view on the table. Despite opposite viewpoints, everyone can acknowledge these statements as truths, even though they may not all be ready to admit it at that moment. It also doesn't imply arguing. On the contrary, naming what is present but unspoken has the most impact with the space and time to let it land, when people can witness and accept its inherent truth.

Initial resistance to speaking the truth might be related to the fear that it will slow things down. It will indeed require you to reconsider whether your quick fixes will be effective, but it will also lead to a more sustainable and often faster approach.

Naming is what we will do in every interaction: in our intake conversations, in our diagnostics report meetings, in any of the interventions with an individual executive or a team. It is also a constant when facilitating a constellation. When we are working with representatives in a constellation, we will not ask for stories or interpretations. We are only interested in the facts at that moment. We ask questions like:

- What is happening in your body right now?

- Who can you see in this constellation?

- Who is out of your sight?

- Where is your attention drawn to?

- What is the one move you would like to make?

- After making this move, what is your experience now?

As we were codifying our way of working in different phases of the M&A process, we realized we were mostly following a certain sequence to define where to intervene first.

In the systemic principles, purpose is the first, giving direction to the system, followed by connection and inclusion, and order and occupying one's place, which jointly form the backbone or structure of the organization. Finally, we added the notion of exchange.

In our work, though, we don't necessarily start with purpose. When the structure is unclear, shaky or dysfunctional, no one knows who is accountable for reconfirming the purpose of the new organization. We might put a lot of effort into redefining the purpose and leading principles, but with the wrong team, so we work first on solidifying the structure before redefining purpose, followed by working on a healthy exchange to establish the new organizations' vitality.

At the risk of simplifying complexity into a map, we noticed that we were typically taking this route in our thinking (and sensing) process.

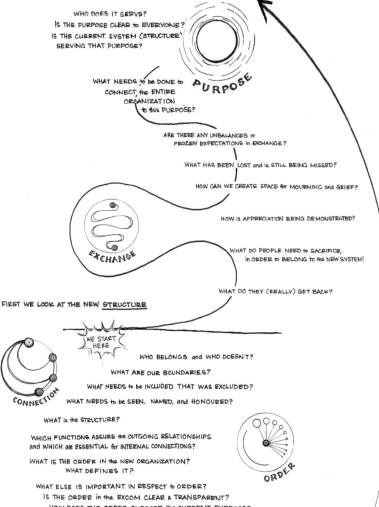

WHAT IS THE NEW PURPOSE?

WHO DOES IT SERVE?
IS THE PURPOSE CLEAR to EVERYONE?
IS THE CURRENT SYSTEM (STRUCTURE)
SERVING THAT PURPOSE?

WHAT NEEDS to be DONE to
CONNECT the ENTIRE
ORGANIZATION
to this PURPOSE?

PURPOSE

ARE THERE ANY UNBALANCES or
FROZEN EXPECTATIONS in EXCHANGE?

WHAT HAS BEEN LOST and is STILL BEING MISSED?

HOW CAN WE CREATE SPACE for MOURNING and GRIEF?

HOW is APPRECIATION BEING DEMONSTRATED?

WHAT DO PEOPLE NEED to SACRIFICE,
in ORDER to BELONG to the NEW SYSTEM?

EXCHANGE

WHAT DO THEY (REALLY) GET BACK?

FIRST WE LOOK AT THE NEW STRUCTURE

WE START
HERE

WHO BELONGS and WHO DOESN'T?

WHAT ARE OUR BOUNDARIES?

WHAT NEEDS to be INCLUDED THAT WAS EXCLUDED?

WHAT NEEDS to be SEEN, NAMED, and HONOURED?

CONNECTION

WHAT is the STRUCTURE?

WHICH FUNCTIONS ASSURE the OUTGOING RELATIONSHIPS
and WHICH are ESSENTIAL for INTERNAL CONNECTIONS?

WHAT IS THE ORDER IN the NEW ORGANIZATION?
WHAT DEFINES IT?

WHAT ELSE IS IMPORTANT IN RESPECT to ORDER?
IS THE ORDER in the EXCOM CLEAR & TRANSPARENT?
HOW DOES THE ORDER SUPPORT the CURRENT PURPOSE?

ORDER

IS EVERYONE in the EXECUTIVE COMMITTEE
TAKING THEIR PLACE and the CORRESPONDING RESPONSIBILITY?
ARE the ROLES (PLACES) DELINEATED and ALLOCATED so that
EVERYONE CAN OWN THEIR OWN ROLE and FEEL ACCOUNTABLE?
IS EVERY DEPARTMENT TAKING their PLACE and the
CORRESPONDING RESPONSIBILITY?

First we look at the new structure. What is included? (Connection and inclusion):

- What is the new identity? Who are you?

- What is the structure?

- What are the key functions in the new system?

- Which ones assure the outgoing relationships and which ones are essential for the internal connections?

- Who belongs and who doesn't?

- What are the boundaries of the system?

- What needs to be included that is excluded now?

- What needs to be seen, named and honoured?

What is the order? (Order and occupying one's place):

- What is the order in the new organization?

- What is it based on? What defines it? What else is important in respect to order?

- What is everyone's place in the system?

- Is the order in the executive committee clear and transparent?

- How do the criteria for order support the current purpose?

- Is there a need for clarifying and/or re-establishing the right order?

Is everyone taking their place? (Order and occupying one's place):

- Is everyone in the executive committee taking their place and the corresponding responsibility? How about the leaders at all levels in the hierarchy?

- Are the roles (places) allocated and delineated so that everyone can take ownership for their own role and assume full accountability?

- Is every department taking its place and the corresponding responsibility?

Is everybody heading to the same 'true north'? (Purpose):

- What is the new purpose?

- How does it differ from the previous ones from the separate companies?

- Who does it serve?

- Is the purpose clear to everyone?

- Is the current system (structure) serving that purpose?

- What needs to be adjusted in the system to really serve the purpose?

- What needs to be done to connect the entire organization to the purpose?

How do you enable vitality in the system? (Exchange):

- Are there any unbalances or frozen expectations?

- What has been lost and is still being missed? How can you create space for mourning and grief?

- How is recognition visible? How is appreciation being demonstrated?

- What do people need to sacrifice to belong to the new system?

- What do they (really) get back?

How to take the first step, and the first next step

We will most often intervene where we get stuck first in this flow. Seldom will we add another detailed implementation plan with multiple swim lanes to the existing integration map, as we have learned throughout the years that it's wise to take the first step and experience how it changes the shape of the system before deciding on the next move. That might feel uncomfortable to start with, especially for strong thinkers and analysts who like to hold on to a two-year plan, but the added value of systemic intelligence is in the navigation tools and the new skillsets. For us as facilitators, it is vital to build a bridge between the familiar technical approach and this adaptive way of working.

Listen to the system's narrative as it is speaking to you in many different ways through the organization's core language; people's exact words; what is being said and not being said; the most urgent problems and dysfunctions, which you will start to see as symptoms rather than diseases. We structure our interventions and reference them with what they are to achieve like this:

- Related to connection and inclusion
  - Including what was excluded
  - Excluding what does not belong anymore
  - Honouring what needs to be seen, named and honoured
- Related to order and occupying one's place
  - Restoring order
  - Occupying one's place and taking the corresponding responsibility
- Related to purpose
  - Defining and connecting to purpose
- Related to exchange
  - Restoring exchange

 Including what was excluded, excluding what does not belong anymore

Exclusion can lead to some of the strongest and most destructive dynamics: internal battles between business units, fundamental breakdowns in the value chain, silent sabotage, mutiny, bullying, etc. But being overly inclusive also has undesirable effects: it often slows down or paralyzes the organization and its decision-making processes. It could create risk aversion and can kill innovation.

Including and excluding are vital movements in an organizational system. To understand what belongs and what doesn't, we refer back to the fundamental question: 'What is the relevant system for this problem or issue we need to solve?' The M&A is the ideal moment to fundamentally redefine what is included and what needs to be excluded. Sometimes this is long overdue in one or both of the organizational systems. One or both might have created an organizational design that is not fit for purpose, just being a combination of well-defined structures with correcting mechanisms (additional departments, special assignments, formal and informal coalitions, short cuts, etc).

This foundational greenfield question is often mistaken for the synergies process, a phase that is often feared because it implies redundancies and potentially lay-offs. Depending on the adjacency of the different parties, you might find yourself on different levels with two people for each role. The synergy targets in the tactical implementation plan are typically focused on combining roles, expanding people's expertise – sales or customer-service reps can easily represent both product portfolios in the market – identifying best practices and saving costs. But from a systemic point of view, we are raising different questions here, for example:

- If this M&A leads you into a new era of biologics, does your existing research and development expertise still belong in the future?

- If your strategic acquisition confirms your aspiration to become the number one in generics, can you still afford all the innovation projects you are currently funding?

- If your spin-off business's major task for survival is to become the lowest cost supplier, is the IT operating model that was designed for high-end innovation and digitalisation still the right one?

- If you are serious about your sustainability plea to the market and community, should the acquisition you just did in the recycling sector get a seat at the executive table?

- If you are committed to making this a merger of equals, how can you include leaders from both legacies at all levels of the organization?

- If new business development is a separate unit in the newly acquired company, how do you make it a part of your core structure without killing its innovative force when you have set a target of 40% revenue to come from newly developed products?

- If you have the historical timeline on the wall, how can you include the rich legacy of the 127-year-old company you just bought beyond marking it with one dot on the day of the acquisition?

- If you are about to embark on a journey of disruptive change, which skill- and mindset needs to be included, and what mindset and behaviour does not belong any longer?

Excluding what does not belong anymore is important to avoid the new system being burdened with an inert structure. As nobody can leave the system unnoticed, the way you decide and execute on this will define whether you can start with a clean and agile vehicle or will trigger other correcting forces.

We sometimes see departments and people who seem to exclude themselves, despite efforts from the rest of the organization to include them. Whenever we see that happening, we immediately ask, 'Are people still connected to something or someone else? Where does their loyalty reside if they cannot connect to the new?'

We realize that the timeframe between the due diligence phase and the actual launch is often too limited to do a complete greenfield exercise. At the same time, it is worth raising some fundamental questions in the executive and implementation teams early on to avoid a tight web of entanglements. The simple act of providing the critical leaders with this systemic lens has a significant impact. We see them asking the right systemic questions and naming what is. By doing so, they gain credibility in their teams and buy time as people understand that an integration process is an extensive process where not everything can be solved immediately.

Honouring what needs to be seen, named and honoured

- Honouring the qualities of the acquired company (even if they lost their credit worth)

- Honouring its roots, founding spirit, successes and strengths

- Honouring the contribution of the people whose jobs have now become redundant as a result of the synergies

- Honouring the attachment of the acquired employees to their previous company

- Honouring the loss of status, position or job

- Honouring the mourning period that people are going through

Honouring does not mean that you feel exactly the same. It does not mean that you approve of what has happened. It implies that you are willing to look at the entire system; to acknowledge what was good or well-intended; to understand that there might be unspoken loyalties, even to a system that was not healthy, not performing, perhaps not ethical.

Remember the company we referred to in the true story 'We missed ourselves, so we bought them'? The company's last acquisition got it on its knees, leading to a massive restructuring, resulting in the loss of 25% of the workforce. Thousands and thousands of people lost their jobs across the globe. The value destruction in the founding country was impressive. Even the national government got involved. The press was pitiless, naming the situation 'a future textbook example of how to destroy value in a two-year timeframe'.

While working with the company's employees in many sites across the world, we saw the mix of emotions in everybody's eyes: anger, fear, frustration, combined with pride, determination, loyalty and a spirit of holding hands. We initially focused on honouring what was there:

- The deeply rooted concern of the founder and subsequent CEOs about the destiny of the founding country

- The entrepreneurial spirit of the founder, who had led the growth from a simple shop to a multibillion-dollar global company

- The vision – the true purpose – of the leadership to make the company's products accessible to all people, both in terms of price and availability

- The employees' pride at seeing the company's products used by their mothers or fathers, spouses or children

And obviously, the emotions related to the earthquake the employees were experiencing at that moment:

- Fear of losing their jobs

- Anger towards the leadership for making the wrong decisions

- Sadness at seeing long-term colleagues leaving

- Relief that they were not (yet) impacted

- Shame because of the press coverage

In JK Rowling's fifth *Harry Potter* book, *The Order of the Phoenix*, Hermione tries to explain to Harry and Ron how their classmate Cho must be feeling after she kissed Harry. As she sums up the myriad of Cho's emotions, including excitement, happiness, confusion, guilt, worry, pain and fear, Ron replies with a stunned look on his face, 'One person can't feel all that at once.' But yes, people can encounter a whole range of strong and mixed emotions when dealing with turbulent times.

When inclusion or honouring are needed to disentangle certain dynamics, we typically work closely with both the leaders and the communication strategists on reinforcing these in broader communications. It is critical to seize the opportunity in the pre- and post-merger phases to rebrand the company's identity, to rewrite the narrative and invite the employees to engage in the new storyline. Many different communication channels can be used to retell the relevant stories of the past, to remind people of the founding history of the acquired company and to put a face to the new names. Obviously, you must guard congruence in the process. It's not about developing a brilliant spin-doctor-like communication and branding campaign that is perceived by the employees as hollow when they don't see leaders' behaviour aligning with their words.

 ## Restoring order and occupying one's place

Restoring order

One of our colleagues handed us this question:

> 'If you were only able to do one thing, what would it be?'

Our answer is 'naming'. Even though it seems like a small intervention, we have countless stories of the impact of naming what is. Our second choice would be 'restoring order'.

In situations with a severe lack of clarity, in times of crisis, in an environment with unhealthy dynamics in the leadership team – be it the executive commit-tee, a local management team or the team in charge of executing the integration plan – all other interven-tions will have a limited effect if order is not restored. We could also phrase it in a positive way: addressing order accelerates all other improvement efforts.

This intervention is not to be underestimated in terms of impact and resistance. A CEO may prefer to start a large and expensive consulting engagement, includ-ing training and coaching for all middle managers, rather than revive their arena experience, openly dis-cuss the current C-suite relations, make some tough decisions and take action accordingly, but not address-ing order can lead to a certain level of paralysis in the team. Team members are careful what they say; not speaking up is chosen over having a healthy opposing point of view.

We will always carefully assess whether the environ-ment is safe enough to address order immediately with the entire team, or whether we need to do some pre-work with the number-one leader.

CASE STUDY: WHO'S FIRST?

A few years ago, we worked with a senior leadership team in a large bank, post-merger and post-restructuring. The leader, who came from the buying party, was known for her determination and thoughtfulness. The executives had given her freedom to decide on the new team composition, only asking her to consider candidates from both legacies.

In our private conversation with her, we asked her this: 'Imagine your next leadership team meeting. If you were to send out invitations to all participants, one by one, what would be the sequence in which you would do so? Who would be the first one who comes to mind? Who's next?'

As she looked at her honest answers, she realized exactly what her team was sensing, but not talking about. Her connection with them was not based on service years, experience level, contribution, magnitude of responsibility or history with the buying or acquired company, but rather on her level of trust.

As she was truly willing to role model self-reflection and openness to look beyond first and second impressions, we were able to name the order in front of the entire team. During an off-site meeting, where we spent the first day establishing psychological safety and an environment of trust, we set up the room with the two ends representing both legacy companies, inviting people to find their own place in between their previous company and the new identity.

Interestingly enough, the door was right in the middle, so the two people who had been hired to join the new company were standing in the doorway. The leader stood in the centre of the room, inviting all the other participants one by one, in her sequence, to join her team, saying, 'You were the first, second, third person I thought of to invite on to my team. You have a place in this team, based on your contributions and role in... I have known you personally since... and what I value about you is...' For some, the last sentence was, 'I don't know you well, but I am willing to invest time in getting to know you and establishing our relationship' or 'I realize that we've had some conflicts in the past and I am committed to finding out where we stand right now.'

It was daring and beautiful – daring because there was a risk that people would feel rejected and take her words too personally. Some of you may remember being chosen last to join sports teams in school. We wanted to avoid the new team members feeling any sense of rejection, so we made sure we created the circumstances for everyone to experience this exercise in a safe way.

We concluded the team intervention with a facilitated discussion on order. Given the organization's current post-merger challenges, we saw a need to define what the criteria were to set the order in this team, in this moment. Even though there were some heated discussions as the team members chose honest and straight talk over sugar-coating, every single person felt seen and respected, although their place in the order may not have been the one they'd envisioned.

As a final step, we asked the new leadership team members to line up in the order they had decided upon and sense what this order did to them as an individual contributor to the team, and to the team as a whole. We stopped talking and invited them to start sensing. One of the leaders, who had been expressing doubts in the early part of the discussion, had the clear sensation while standing in line that this was exactly the order that would strengthen the whole system, at the same time benefiting him in his new role.

Naming their reality, spending time allowing for connection or reconnection, and re-establishing order was critical for the participants to start the journey as a new team and had a tremendous influence on the trust within the team. They found ways to deal with conflicts behind closed doors and align before communicating to the organization. The employees saw a leadership team speaking with one voice, painting an integrated vision, building a narrative of inclusion and value for the strengths of both the acquiring company and the one that had been bought.

This was obviously not the end for this team. The systemic principles are dynamic. As their initial integration work came to an end, they were tasked to focus on interregional growth which required them to 'reorder'. After the critical phase of building a new organization, the next phase required a stronger outward movement. For their effectiveness, it was critical they identified the new functional order that would be of most service in this next step. This shifted the focus to the more outgoing roles: the sales and marketing department; the public affairs function; the customer services teams.

One of the experts in the area of family and organizational constellations, Jan Jacobs Stam, refers to these two movements as 'communio' and 'agens'. Within an organization there are critical roles that foster community and weave the internal connections, represented by the Latin word *communio* (from the verb *communire*, which means to strengthen and to barricade). In Eastern traditions they would refer to this inward focus as the feminine principle of bonding and hosting (Yin). Other roles are focused on the outside world, the forward and outward movement, establishing a place in the market and facing competition, reflected in the Latin word *agens* (from the verb *agere*, which means to act) – the masculine energy of entering into action (Yang). When referring to feminine and masculine, we are talking about archetypal energies, not about gender. Both men and women can thrive in any and both energies.

Inward- and outward-focused movements are critical for the survival of any system and the CEO of a company is accountable for safeguarding both. What the team in our case study recognized well was that their growth ambition had been jeopardized by their lack of connection. Without losing sight of their customers and competitors, they worked first to build the community within the team. As their growth plans became more actionable, the team order and composition had to change again to tap into a different skillset. People with a career path in multiple regions and a track record of growth in unknown territories were critical for this next step.

In general, all systems have an intrinsic order. In that respect, the outward-focused roles and functions come before the inward-focused ones in the order. Without the organization looking outward, there might not even be a need to create a business community to make it happen. This doesn't make either of the roles more or less important; it is just about confirming the typical order that strengthens the healthy

EMERGENT

survival of the system. Naming and confirming that order grounds the entire system and everyone in it.

When working with public companies, we sometimes see entanglements in the order between the board of directors and the office of chief executives, especially after a merger or acquisition when the CEO of one of the legacies is appointed to be the new CEO and the other one gets a seat on the board, so both are still influencing their former allies. The board of directors has a clear mandate to oversee and supervise the companies' activities. The moment it starts intervening in the day-to-day decision making and bypassing the CEO, it actually leaves its place. By doing so, the board members are not only stepping on the toes of the executive leaders, they are also leaving their own critical roles vacant.

Often, we facilitate a physical intervention to restore the order in an executive team by seating all members in the right order in the conference room for the critical decision-making discussions. In some countries, societal or organizational cultures, this order is obvious. Think about the well-thought-through seating at a royal banquet, or the ranked seating in armed forces according to attendees' stars and stripes. In other societies or companies, it is almost taboo to mention or confirm order. It is seen as politically incorrect or going against the core values of respect for people.

We are strongly focused on connection and inclusion in systemic work, yet an 'orderless' system creates confusion and unhealthy dynamics. Inclusion does not work without order. Inclusion is not about forming one happy bunch of people where everyone has an equal seat at every table; it is about defining the right order for the system to achieve its purpose.

CASE STUDY: REARRANGING THE ORDER

We were working with a European company at the edge of global expansion. Driven by one of its core values, its aim was to not overcomplicate things; to unclutter processes and decide with speed and agility. But the reality was showing the exact opposite. As the company culture was strong on inclusion, it resulted in many meetings with many people, leading to extensive approval processes with even more meetings. This inclusive approach led to high engagement scores, low turnover, a friendly atmosphere and strong results in the first twenty years of the company's existence.

At the turning point in the company's history, when the leaders were courting potential partners to form joint ventures or acquire key players all around the world, the company culture was getting in the way of fast decision making, innovative thinking, risk taking and resource planning: all essential attributes given its inorganic growth strategy. With this executive team, it was critical to rearrange the order. To identify which regions or departments needed to be involved in the growth work stream and which ones needed to stay focused on running the day-to-day business in Europe. This implied excluding some executive leaders from the decision-making processes around acquisitions and integration plans, not for the sake of it, but to reconfirm their position and include them in the matters that required their full attention. We kept reminding them to define what the relevant system was for the challenge at hand. Their careful consideration of which table they were talking about and who – by nature of their role and skillset – needed to have a seat at it was automatically cascaded down to the entire organization, empowering others at lower levels to do exactly the same.

Occupying one's place and taking on the corresponding responsibility

Having an impressive title or a detailed job description doesn't necessarily mean that people are behaving accordingly and taking the responsibility that comes with it. Some leaders show up physically but are mentally absent. Others will hide behind multiple distractions so that they don't have to face their real leadership mandate.

A CEO obviously has a strong outward-focused role, dealing with the board, the shareholders, the stock market, political leaders and government agencies, the press, competitors and communities. That doesn't give them an excuse to forget about their role as the number one inside the organization. The opposite is equally valid – no organizational system works in isolation, so a focus solely on the internal system is not sustainable.

When executives are leaving their places empty, others will automatically step into their shoes, leading not only to internal competition and conflict between individuals, but also to those others leaving their seats empty in turn. This creates a negative cascading effect. We also see technically oriented managers who feel most comfortable in the details and micromanage the team members reporting to them, sometimes even the layers below. In essence, they too are not occupying their own seat; they have one foot in the position of their team, disabling their staff to lead and supervise effectively. At the same time, they are limiting development opportunities for their people by constantly intervening in their operational and decision-making processes. Their entanglement causes conflict, so we often advise them to get out of the way. There is a time when a leader's efforts to help are counterproductive.

To be able to take one's place, it is important everyone knows exactly what that place is, and then connects with it and fully occupies it. No stepping into someone else's shoes. An organization can handle an employee assuming someone else's role for a short period of time, but only if it is fully transparent that it is temporary, and that whatever formal or informal solution they install is an interim one.

When all take their place, there is rest and flow in the system. This may sound like a rigid stick-to-your-job-description message, but it is not. It is a call for a robust and transparent structure that is able to hold the multitude of transactions – be they financial, physical or relational – that make up an enterprise. It is a plea for leaders to be fully in charge.

 Purpose

Mission and purpose are not the same. The mission statement defines what the company wants to become. It is often stated in terms of market share, market position, geographical presence, organic and inorganic growth potential, in some cases combined with corporate social responsibility pledges related to the environmental footprint. Purpose goes beyond that. Purpose probes for the real added value to society. What do your customers need your organization to be? What real need are you fulfilling? What have you been invited to? How does your organization contribute to the larger system? Purpose is the answer to a societal question, even if that question has not been expressed yet, not to a made-up need.

A true purpose statement will be lived by the leaders and employees and embraced by all other stakeholders: the clients you are serving; the suppliers in your value chain; the communities you are in; the legislative authorities. For longer-term sustainability, purpose has to evolve and regular realignment is key.

CASE STUDY: WHAT IS SOCIETY INVITING US TO?

In our work with a national retail company, including the acquisition of an equally-renowned retailer in another segment, we discovered that the answer to this question had been clear 100 years ago, but required a fundamental rethink for this century.

Back in the olden days, the eldest son of the founder had radical new ideas. Not only related to the purpose of his father's small business, but also concerning the employers-employees relationship and its impact on financial results and long-term success. Unlike most company leaders in the aftermath of the second industrial revolution, he abandoned the paternalistic concept and created a partnership structure for all employees, which included better working conditions and a profit-sharing scheme. His father didn't welcome his revolutionary plans at first but allowed him to try it out in one of the stores. As he was quickly able to turn a loss-making shop into a profitable one, his father capitulated.

The company-wide partnership was a fact and served as an economical case study much beyond the country's border. Partners were wearing their stake as a badge of honour, resulting in lifelong loyalty and service from most of them. Interestingly enough, when looking at the customer base, we saw the same lifelong loyalty there – 70% of the company's revenue came from recurrent customers who were honouring the stores' excellent product assortment, quality and returns policy, and the staff's friendliness and service-oriented mindset.

When diagnosing the current culture across the company, we observed that it was consistently marked by compliance with the guidelines of the mothership. The partnership structure no longer led to local freedom to operate, innovation or creative problem solving; governance had grown disproportionally to keep everybody happy. In addition to this, the market conditions had changed significantly over the last decade. More and more consumers were finding their way to online shopping and other retailers or companies with totally new business models. This new reality created a feeling of threat in the entire organization and led to a certain paralysis in the local stores. Over the years, the organization had lost connection with the founding spirit.

When working with different levels of leaders, walking them through the history and pivotal points of the organization, they realized that it was not the form or the structure of the partnership that was keeping them hostage. In fact, the opposite was true. They started to understand that these principles were supporting what they needed at this moment, namely the space and energy to innovate.

In our forums with all leaders, we reconnected them to the founding spirit, the initial purpose, by getting them to ask themselves, 'Are we a partnership in the first place and then a retail company, or the other way around? What is the impact of the answer to that question? How can we master this new context? The first founding generations were entrepreneurial and visionary, so how can we reignite those qualities in the current organization?'

Different external and internal forces can trigger the need to reconsider your purpose. In our experience of successful centenarian companies, all the employees know the founder's story, founding principles and initial purpose. At the same time, these companies have been agile enough to adjust their purpose along the way without losing connection to their roots.

Recommended read

An interesting read about long-lasting companies is *Built to Last: Successful habits of visionary companies* by Jim Collins and Jerry Porras.

Many renowned companies have fundamentally shifted their purpose and moved into completely different industries over time. It is essential in such a substantial identity shift to consider the other systemic principles and ask yourself whether you need to:

- Reconnect the organization to the redefined purpose.

- Reconsider who belongs to the new system and who no longer does. What are you focused on? What are you not doing anymore? What is the impact of this prioritization/de-prioritization?

- Rethink the criteria for order.

- Reflect on the impact on exchange during the transition period and beyond.

Exchange

Exchange is the juice that creates vitality in a system. It makes sure that the system can sustain itself in the long run without a constant external injection of energy, investment or acquisitions.

Energy is about movement, so the notion of exchange needs to be considered in a dynamic way. It is not about settling the debit and credit accounts at all times. It is not about finding a constant break-even point. It is not about giving and expecting an immediate equal return on your efforts. It is about being able to continuously sense and understand what 'the ask' really is, and what you are giving in return. It is dynamic and active, circling around an ever-moving balance.

Mid- and long-term systematic imbalance in exchange will lead to unplanned and unwanted restoring mechanisms. It creates a leakage of energy, resulting in a corporate or department-specific lethargy, resistance and visible or invisible dysfunction.

Have you ever wondered why employees are paid in arrears at the end of the month rather than before they start the work? The founders of a company were the first ones to do the giving. They invested money, time and energy into a new business; they took risks. In that sense, employees start with a debt to the founders, and later on to the owners or shareholders. They then give – hours of work, dedication, focus, ideas, etc – before being paid.

CASE STUDY: THE FULL STORY BEHIND THEFT

We facilitated a constellation with a senior vice president (SVP) after the company she represented terminated the contract of a long-term employee – a trusted and hardworking expert who was caught falsifying his travel expense reports over a period of six months. He was dismissed for misconduct and was immediately escorted to the exit.

The SVP came to one of our organizational constellation days to bring this case to the group, as she did not want to simply accept the investigation conclusions that were marking this once-valued employee as a thief. She wanted to understand the company's contribution to the situation, and realized that there would be a delayed and possibly hidden effect on his team and the broader organization. In other words, she intuitively knew that his conscious decision to claim more money may have been a symptom of something larger.

The constellation revealed a long-lasting imbalance between what the company asked from its employees and what it was offering them in return. Representatives of the employees in the constellation systematically testified to both their loyalty to the company and its purpose, and complete exhaustion. The company had gone through a prolonged period of crisis management, leading to fewer and fewer resources, both in terms of people and investment money. On the other hand, demands on the remaining resources increased year on year.

The man who had been fired was an esteemed member of a global support team, travelling around the world and regularly sacrificing private time to leave on Sundays. About one year ago, there had been a further cut into the travel allowances. Contrary to the way he'd reacted to previous cost restrictions, this man no longer raised his voice and continued to dutifully perform his role. As others looked to him as a role model, they too accepted the continued crisis mode. As a result, the cost-saving measure was considered to have been successfully implemented by the top leadership team.

Another contributing factor to the imbalance was the lack of strong performance management in the company. It might sound like a paradox, but the company's foundation was built on a high value for people, leading to an amicable culture. As the leaders tended to avoid difficult conversations with low performers, most of the extra work was loaded on to the strong performers – the ones who were already going the extra mile.

There was no way that the dismissal could be undone – that would undermine the implementation and reinforcement of the company's code of conduct, and make this man's position impossible in the team. Instead, the SVP left the constellation day with the following plan:

- To withdraw from legal charges against the employee
- To invite him for a respectful and holistic exit interview
- To hold focus group discussions with the teams to listen to their voice around exchange

- To reconsider certain compensation and benefits elements as a result of these roundtables
- To explore other ways of recognizing and developing people within the low-margins constraint
- To keep the communication lines open around employee engagement and concerns through regular pulse checks

---

Specifically in an M&A situation, where people will be sensitive and sometimes even searching for any sign of 'loss', it is vital to keep an eye on exchange at all times, while managing expectations and communicating in a transparent way. Sometimes the loss is real, but – for solid business reasons – will not be compensated for, at least not in monetary ways. Developing a strong narrative about the bigger picture and the broader systemic exchange over the long term will support people in settling their own balance or give them the opportunity to decide to leave.

We will elaborate on the notion of exchange in M&As later in this chapter.

We also see examples of company cultures and habits where what employees are receiving is disconnected from their actual contribution to the results. For example, this often happens in strongly unionized environments where the current compensation scheme is an accumulation of decades of collective labour agreements, and not connected to the current reality anymore. We have seen maintenance crews going home at 4pm, knowing that their job was not finished, only to be 'called in' fifteen minutes after arriving home so they could add the significant call-in compensation to the overtime they were doing. We've read articles about members of national parliaments claiming their attendance fees while not showing up, or reporting present for two minutes just to walk out right away. We have seen leaders getting a totally out-of-context representation allowance. We see outdated systems for promotion and yearly salary increases, mostly based on the amount of years an employee has been in the company rather than merit, quality of work or achievements. All these examples influence the vitality of the system, including the system's environment.

When an imbalance gives too much to the employees, unrelated to their time, effort and commitment, you might expect people to raise the bar for themselves and others, but often the opposite is true. Employees feel entitled to what they have and entitled to receive even more, as if they have accumulated more rights simply because they've always done so before. This implies that they expect to be compensated for any additional task, process change or request for flexibility. The organization becomes dependent and demonstrates a 'helplessness that has been taught or acquired'.

There is obviously a need to create stability and a structured framework for a company's compensation and benefits strategy, following a country's legislative requirements. Employees have a need to adjust their personal balance sheet and their private lives to what they earn.

In recent years, we have seen organizational models in many industries evolving towards network structures with freelance engagements, but the systemic principles also apply in an environment like this. It is interesting to consider how the principles of connection and inclusion, order and occupying one's place, and exchange are established and honoured in a more open, flexible and dynamic organizational system.

Recommended read

An interesting read about this evolution in organization forms is *Reinventing Organizations: A guide to creating organizations inspired by the next stage of human consciousness* by Frederic Laloux.

Certainly, the compensation for people's time, activities, dedication and contribution to the results goes beyond financial returns and fringe benefits. It includes connection to a company's reputation, brand and market, individual and team growth and development opportunities, collaboration with colleagues, mentoring, skill building, exposure to other countries or cultures, a sense of purpose, and many more things specific to individuals. An element we always see included in our work around exchange is respect

– difficult to quantify, but easy to measure when you practise deep listening.

We remember working with a bank post-merger. The employees of the acquired company were saying, 'We feel like we were loaded into a truck at our location, transported and unloaded at our destination (the new acquiring company's location).' It had hit them hard. Even when all objective elements of the integration are successful, if the employees feel they have not been treated with respect and dignity, the employer will be in their debt for quite a while. Employees will (usually unconsciously) expect compensation or recognition, and only when they get it will they show their full potential at work. Only then can vitality increase.

The notion of exchange is a sensitive one in the aftermath of a merger or acquisition. There is often already a fragile balance in exchange before the merger, aggravated by the typical pre-merger measures, only to become fluid for a certain period of time after the merger. The new normal is unclear and all individuals are carefully scanning the horizon for 'What is in it for me?'

With a sense of loss already prevailing, leaders are sometimes reluctant to upset people even more, so they use the movement of 'giving' as a compensating mechanism for lack of clarity or entanglements in the systemic principles. Rather than using the new beginning as an opportunity for setting some unhealthy dynamics straight – and we mean straight in a systemic way, not suppressing the symptoms – companies accumulate both systems. Instead of fundamentally rethinking the compensation structure, they choose one of the unbalanced ones, or a combination of both previously used by the legacy companies. Initially the latter choice may seem like the best of both worlds for the employees, but adding up two compensation schemes that were ill-constructed to start with leads to an unaffordable situation over the long term. Wages become prohibitively expensive, which threatens the financial health and legitimacy of certain sites or countries.

Compensating employees of the acquired party with a welcome gesture will have a negative impact on the employees of the acquirer. Leaving employees of the acquirer with a compensation scheme that benefits them over the others will create unrest and a sense of unfairness. Creating (giving) special assignments or temporary roles that don't contribute anything to the new purpose will distort the organizational health.

Marrying two companies with a fundamentally different background of compensation and career progression dynamics will require the joined leadership to rethink their system from scratch. Employees from each party might value fundamentally different things. Often money cannot compensate for other cultural traits. Employees who thrived in an environment where there was creativity, out-of-the box thinking, risk taking and personal growth will not be seduced by a higher pay scheme and bonus system when they feel restricted in a highly corporate, boxed environment.

Sometimes the water is too deep between the two organizational systems, in which case it is wise for them to consider a merger model that keeps the different companies separate from each other.

All our interventions around exchange include the impacted audience, as exchange is not a black-and-white matter that can be calculated and equalled out on an excel spreadsheet. It requires leaders' intentions to be transparent, constantly exploring fairness, competitiveness and a sense of reality in the area of giving and receiving. It demands a high sense of personal responsibility from all involved. Whether exchange is balanced is often perceived on an individual level, based on each employee's own expectations, values, beliefs and personal life situation. It is impossible for company leaders to accommodate all these different needs individually. It requires the first-line supervisors, who are closest to the teams, to keep an eye on everyone's balance sheet.

Obviously, a corporate environment expects people to perform and strive for great results. At the same time, it is good to be aware of the myriad ways you can balance and rebalance the give and take in the organization. Transparency around what there is to receive and what there is to give in an organizational system comes with the personal accountability of each and every individual, whether they sign up for what is on the table or not. Obviously, there needs to be both formal (through works councils and HR processes) and informal opportunities for employees to raise concerns related to exchange, yet we invite them to maintain their personal power at all times. It is their responsibility to evaluate the compatibility between their own and the organization's values. To set clear boundaries for themselves. To decide at pivotal moments whether there's still a good match between their values and the new way of working, and whether they want to stay or leave.

Not deciding or acting comes at a cost for both the individual and the team. Moments of frustration or struggle will be a part of everyone's professional path, but staying in a troubled professional relationship for a long time will lead to disempowerment and unhealthy invisible entanglements.

Unsurprisingly, an M&A is often one of these pivot points in people's careers. Employees were initially attracted to one company and now they are confronted with another one with different values, a faster or slower pace, new written and unwritten rules, another market reputation and – on a systemic level – different criteria that define order. They may be required to act differently in order to be included, being faced with a slightly or completely redefined workplace and different dynamics of exchange. At a certain moment, when the initial fluidity of the post-merger phase is over and the identity of the newly formed organization has been crystallized, it is critical for each employee to decide whether they still belong or not. If the answer is no, if the consequences of adapting are too great, it is better for employee and employer to part and go their separate ways.

As a result, people leaving after an M&A is not necessarily a bad thing. In fact, expect some to leave, but when you see all your talented, high-potential people running for the door, screaming, look at the underlying systemic dynamics to safeguard the future. The diagnostics table we presented in Chapter Five can support you in identifying the most impactful levers to turn the situation around.

Recommended read

William Bridges in his book *Managing Transitions: Making the most of change* gives an interesting view on dealing with transitions. His book is closely aligned with the systemic approach. He dives deeper into the feelings of loss and what people have to let go of.

A True Story:
If Only The Supervisors Would...

'If only the supervisors would understand their responsibility as gatekeepers.'

We come in four years after the acquisition. She is leading one of the global functions. We meet her in the organization's impressive headquarters in an exclusive area of town. She joined the company around the time of the acquisition and has no strong attachment to either of the two legacy parties.

She wants our advice on how to achieve a fundamental mindset shift in the lowest level of the hierarchy. Her one-page framework for the critical role of the first-line supervisor is a process flow chart that guides them through their typical working day. According to her framework, they are supposed to be the gatekeepers for all operational performance criteria. They should release their workers for duty upon arrival. They have to predict the day, perform risk assessments at each stage and act accordingly.

There are 180,000 people, more than 10,000 of them supervisors, in this newly formed, horizontally integrated company, which consists of a trading partner and an industrial processor. The two legacy companies are determined to integrate and identify and apply best practices. One had strong processes in place: high-quality standards and guidelines, execution and auditing processes, leading to good operational discipline in the organization. The other had a different approach, developing good practices in a centre-of-excellence model and leaving the regions and sites free to implement them. The organization then held each site accountable for the results, not for the way it got them. The approach of the newly formed company is a compromise: it has adopted the high-quality standards from one but presents them as guiding principles.

Following her request, we suggest scheduling a first focus group discussion with a selected group of operations and functional leaders. All regions are represented in the room. There is a lot of talking about assessment results and job descriptions; performance reviews and variable compensation for leaders and supervisors; investment in skills training. The discussion stays on a theoretical level until we decide

– unannounced – to use a constellation technique to understand the real dynamics. We put the three most obvious layers – workforce, first-line supervisor, operations managers – on the table using cups, then paint several scenarios. Have the supervisors grown up through the ranks, which may make it difficult for them to enforce behaviour that they didn't demonstrate themselves? Are the operations managers micromanaging, pushing the supervisors out of their roles? Are the operations managers focusing on something else and leaving a leadership gap?

While we are painting the scenarios, we move the cups back and forth to reflect whatever we are describing. In a few minutes we have the real situation on the table. Most of the operations managers have temporary assignments, but they are not adopting their role for the short period of time they are there, so they feel they are standing at the sidelines. As a result, the operations managers are not shielding the supervisors when they are trying to enforce the standards and rules set by the new global corporate office in their shifts. Because of the confirmed 'guideline' approach, the operations managers are constantly taking the route of least resistance, but adherence to standards is rapidly declining.

The second insight is not necessarily linked to the acquisition but is relevant to understand the supervisors' position. In the communities this organization operates in, tribal leaders have a strong influence.

Their position as employees is, on paper, exactly the same as the other workers', but in the communities that surround the large sites, they have a leading or counselling role in the tribes. And their influence doesn't end as far as the workers are concerned when they all enter the gates at the beginning of the shift. The tribal leaders among the workers are the ones who have the real power, not the supervisors.

These insights shift our focus and approach:

- We focus on clarifying the new operational model and the mandatory corporate standards

- We work with all the leaders, wherever they are in the line of command, to get their act together and decide which standards are mandatory and must be implemented rigorously from the top down and where to allow local freedom and customization

- We set the KPIs accordingly and synchronize the rituals, from the shift hand-over meeting to the top-level performance reviews

- We strengthen the supervisory skills while assuring the supervisors will have a strong back-up from their operations manager

- We engage the entire organization in the why of the best practices and listen to their voices

Questions for reflection

- After an M&A, did you take an element from one legacy company's system and implant it in the other system, without considering how it is connected to other aspects, processes, cultural traits?

- Are the vision, the narrative and the tactics of the newly formed company cascaded down to each level of the organization?

- Are leaders behaving according to their place in the organization?

- Who are the ones with the true power?

7
The Role Of Leaders In A Complex Environment

'We are a constant updating process of the
system that we live in.'
—Thomas Hübl

Setting the stage

'Show me the children and I'll tell you how the
parents are relating to each other.'

Is that true? Yes and no.

One of our initial assumptions is that leaders have a
significant influence on their teams. As a result, we
assume that the organization's performance and culture are a reflection of the leaders – their presence,

their decisions, their words, what they do and what they don't do.

As part of our diagnostics and ongoing consulting work with executive teams, we hold up a mirror to make leaders aware of what they are creating in the organization. Yet after working in different industries for more than twenty years, looking at our clients through a systemic lens, we simply cannot deny that in most cases, there are stronger systemic forces at play overruling the individual leaders' best intentions. Forces that date back to before the current leaders' tenure. Forces that may have been unwillingly created as a survival or correcting mechanism.

In other words, the system is leading.

It is worth repeating that concept to let it sink in.

The system is leading.

This is why it is so critical to see not only the reflection of individual leaders in the mirror, but also the underlying dynamics in the entire system, created by historical events, entanglements and violations towards the systemic principles. The system's restoring mechanisms are often stronger than the individual willpower of a highly capable leader or leadership team. If they don't make the correct diagnosis, they will find themselves fighting windmills.

Does that mean that we don't need a captain on the ship? Does that mean that these highly paid top guys and girls are merely performing a ceremonial role? Quite the contrary. We need men and women who see the deeper layers underneath the drama on the surface. Leaders who are capable of including the company's historic pain. Conscious captains who are willing to acknowledge that their leadership legacy will not depend on some heroic solo effort, but a thoughtful and wise collaboration with the organizational system. Visionaries who are interested in setting up the company for future success, probably long after their temporary role in a long lineage of leaders.

These are the leaders who embrace the systemic lens, who ask the deeper questions and are courageous enough to accept the answers and act upon them. As a result, they turn around seemingly struggling businesses and teams, resolve longstanding issues, inject new creativity and inspiration, and restore energy and flow into the company, only to do it all over again as external and internal influences continuously invite them to reconsider the purpose and leading principles, redefine who and what is needed, rethink order and keep an eye on the notion of exchange. With or without inorganic growth, with or without mergers, acquisitions, divestitures, spin-offs, joint ventures and different kinds of partnership, when you're leading a living organizational system, it's a never-ending task to keep sensing and navigating.

Our interactions and interventions with the executive team, strategic planning team or tactical integration team start with, but are in no way limited to, the theoretical insights about the systemic principles and how they are playing out in the organization at hand, following the diagnostics phase. Knowing and understanding the dynamics in the relevant system on an intellectual level is only the first step and, in some cases, not even necessary to change them. What we really want to do is transform these insights into embodied wisdom. How can we make them fully land in the system, both in the leaders themselves and in the organizational fabric? How can we enable a movement that was initiated by a restoring mechanism of the system in response to a traumatic event or a violation of the system's natural principles to complete its cycle, so that the patterns do not have to be repeated over and over again?

What does it require from the leader?

As we became more and more curious about why certain entanglements were present in one organization and not in the one next door, we realized the enormous opportunity to work with the current leaders and teams, even to restore some of the entanglements or dynamics that had originated several generations ago. We believe that the system is represented in the leader, and by extension everyone who belongs to the system. In our experience, some organizational dynamics resonate with the leader's unintegrated personal triggers. This may seem like a bold statement at first sight, but we have seen it confirmed over and over again. When there are no personal triggers, the leader has absolute clarity related to a specific problem. When he or she has full clarity, the issue does not arise anymore.

We regularly find leaders and teams in stormy weather. Sometimes they try to convince us and themselves that they are in control, but when we take a deeper look, it becomes clear that they are up to their necks in the flood. They feel the underlying current pulling them in different directions; increasing their effort doesn't result in a course correction.

In a hurricane, the famous eye only starts to develop at a certain wind speed. It forms a cylindrical shape that extends up and above the storm, allowing atmospheric air to sink down inside it, acting like a vortex that feeds air into the force of the storm. How can we get a leadership team into the eye of the storm, where they will be able to rise above the hectic perceived reality and bring fresh air and new positive perspectives into the game? How do we get a leader into a zone where they may not feel completely calm, but have enough space to observe the real dynamics in their organization? From that place, they can witness how they are interfering with the system, and in some cases contributing to or even exacerbating it. How can facilitators, coaches and consultants serve the system by creating and holding that place when the leader's capacity to do so is temporarily restricted? How can we rearrange the system within the leadership, leading to an external expression of that shift into the organization? How can we get leaders to balance their outward-going energy, focused on critical stakeholders, owners, headquarters, the customers and the community, and the inward and bonding energy that keeps the organization together in a post-integration phase?

CASE STUDY: WE START ANEW

We were fascinated by the leadership history of a company after two important acquisitions, both with cumbersome integrations. The current capable and strong-willed country CEO was the fourth one in the last eighteen months. Each of the previous CEOs had made significant changes in the executive committee, resulting in a total lack of continuity in most of the critical functional areas.

The first CEO had been well-established in the role for quite some time and was known and trusted by the teams across the country. The country subsidiary he was leading within the larger global company was relatively small. With the organization's acquisition of that country's number one in its industry, soon followed by the addition of a range of assets from another competitor, he found himself in a totally new playing field. The small fish was being asked to swallow a much larger one, and he was assessed as not being the right man for the job. He became the second in command, reporting to a newly appointed CEO from abroad.

This second CEO was moved out of his previous assignment to free up space for another leader, and as a result started the critical and highly challenging integration phase in his new role with little interest in or appetite for the job. He was not close to the country teams and culture, did not understand the specifics of the different parties, delegated the tough integration task to a young and inexperienced project leader, and was faced with extremely tight deadlines and synergy targets. This all resulted in several poor integration decisions that left the employees of both the acquired party – previously cheered as the number-one brand in the industry – and the acquiring party – previously accustomed to high-quality standards and highly performing systems – totally exhausted, frustrated and fearful.

When the disastrous financial results became undeniable, the second CEO was fired and replaced by a third one, hired externally based on excellent industry knowledge and a proven track record of results. Upon arrival, he was shocked by the state he found the business in.

His leadership approach was to build community first. He invested time in increasing trust in his executive committee, installed weekly management meetings lasting a whole day, and started putting the basic processes in place. The organization praised him for his common-sense human approach. He added a layer of protection and defended his organization to the headquarters, but he had already decided by his second month to give up and resign.

When we enter this organization, we meet with the new CEO – number four – the moment she completes her first six months with relative success. The last weeks have showed positive results, compared to the previous loss-making months. Even though she admits she wasn't prepared for this seemingly insurmountable peak, she decided to roll up her sleeves upon arrival and get to work.

The executive team composition at that moment was:

- A CEO, six months in the job
- A strong CFO, a well-known and highly regarded former colleague of the CEO whom she had hired in her first week in her role
- Two functional leaders with a lot of years of service in the acquired brand – the acquisition and integration thereafter left them feeling undervalued, exhausted and even humiliated
- An HR director hired just before the acquisition, who was still catching her breath after the sequence of acquisitions and the following restructurings, tough union negotiations and significant lay-offs
- Five functional leaders, all recently hired, most of them former colleagues of the CEO, who joined the company mainly because they wanted to work with her once more

The CEO is action-oriented. She manages the owners – the third private equity company in a row – and the headquarters (a clear agens focus). She also mandates busloads of consultants to assess and benchmark all critical processes against industry best in class. She drives change fiercely and closely follows up on all results. She and the CFO split the focus areas and are leading the rest of the executive committee in a one-to-one process.

There has been no time for the leadership team to get to know each other. The moment we arrive, we realize there is no sense of team at all.

The voice of the organization was silenced during the first crisis months of the M&A. The CEO has stated that as of now, it is a new company. She doesn't want to hear anyone defending legacy processes or sentiments. None of the three previous CEOs was successful, so this is a breaking point in the history.

'We start anew,' she says.

Even though all the executive committee members confirm that the CEO is the right one for the job, and most of them are inspired by her leadership, that image is not cascaded down into the organization. The employees in the field, who are in desperate need of some inspiration and perspective, don't know her at all. When asked about their top leader, they report that she is just a name for them, sending them a continuous stream of emails with instructions, orders and procedural changes. It has been almost impossible for them to get behind the new leader.

The system will not forget about its past and will not allow the leadership team to erase it completely, at least not before acknowledging what happened and setting a few things straight. The moment you try to exclude past events that have not been integrated, the organization will find ways to help you remember.

When facilitating a constellation, what we are actually doing – besides working on and with the deeper systemic level – is bringing an inner image, consciously or subconsciously present in a leader's mind, out into the room and shining a light on it to observe, take it in, listen to the different voices, and sense from there what the next move needs to be. We make the invisible visible, the implicit explicit.

There is no use in intervening in the organizational system without working with the inner landscape of the leader(s): the way the organization is alive in them; the visible and invisible dynamics and conflicts in them; their beliefs and core needs. This requires the leader to display an inner capacity beyond the skills and competencies that may have made them successful so far. It is not just about industry knowledge, business expertise and execution of strategies. Today's complexity demands much more. It demands the capacity to deal with ambiguity, with 'not knowing', and it will include discomfort. It requires a leader to be able to hold space for themselves and their teams so that reflective learning and fundamental mindset shifts can take place. It needs them to pause at the right moment; to enter into stillness and spaciousness instead of jumping to conclusion and actions; to allow the questions and answers to emerge; to invite and live through motions and emotions. It requires a previously unseen inner versatility.

The more we ask different questions, intended to bring the systemic dynamics to the surface, the more we get new questions from leaders, and the more we see them inviting those questions from their teams. Let's reflect on some of those questions now.

Systemic questions

What will the consequences of your decisions be for generations to come?

When holding community meetings around the children's fire, native peoples ask themselves, 'How will this decision affect the seven generations to come?' Imagine what our planet would look like, what our communities and families would feel like, if we considered the long-term impact of everything we did.

How often do you rely on or hide behind your technical and functional knowledge and expertise?

How often do you admit that you simply don't know? That the solution to this question is beyond your current reach? That it will require a totally different mindset?

We were recently facilitating a three-day top-150 conference for a large plastics manufacturer. While we were talking about the circular economy and the complex challenge of plastic littering and plastic recycling, the CEO openly expressed in front of his extended leadership team:

> 'I came to admit to myself that, as much as I think about this challenge, as much as I try to map all the ins and outs, as much as I lose sleep over it, as much as I feel responsible for solving this for our community and our children, the solution will not come from me as an individual, as brilliant a thinker as I might consider myself from time to time. This truly complex question will require a cross-fertilization between different industries, between different generations. It requires us to be open to solutions we have not even considered, suggestions from people we have not asked yet.'

Do you trust your gut?

Do you trust your intuition? Your inner voice? Dare you tune in to the organizational system, the teams, your people, realizing that will expose you to more feelings and emotions and tension than you may be used to? Are you willing to truly listen, knowing that implies you have to act accordingly? Are you willing to suspend your brilliant analysis for a new solution that is still unknown to you?

What inner work do you need to do to be able to continue to lead in complexity?

How do you better understand how you function in different systems (family of origin, current family, community, business, etc) so that you are aware of your patterns, triggers, pitfalls, blind spots? How do you avoid leading the organization with one eye only?

How important is it for you to leave 'your' legacy behind? To put your stamp on the organization?

What are you trying to prove? To whom? Do you see yourself as a hero, the one who is saving the day and gets the applause or the bonus for it? Or can you see yourself as one link in a long lineage of leadership?

We were inspired by the Netflix series *Designated Survivor* that made an unknown and unprepared former professor President of the United States. As everyone, including himself, doubts whether he is up for it, he decides to accept the task and commits to lead in an honest and transparent way. It might be a bit naïve to believe he is able to stay authentic and true to himself and his promises, given the never-ending range of roadblocks he is faced with every day, but we found it truly fascinating and inspirational to witness how he held his ground at all times, reverting back to his inner guidance when he got tempted to take a different route.

Do you stand by your values?

In his book *In Over Our Heads*, Robert Kegan claims we can't survive in the current volatile and complex world if we let ourselves be defined by the group norms and expectations. We must let our own values lead the way, even if that puts us outside the group.

What are you loyal to?

The field of systemic intelligence covers the notion of loyalty. Loyalty can totally destabilize a system or create unhealthy dynamics. We see it in different forms.

Most systems have a set of unwritten rules that define what it takes to belong. The ones who don't follow those get excluded. Strong loyalty leads people to go along with the rules, even when they aren't in line with their own values, or are destructive, unethical or illegal.

Employees can demonstrate visible or invisible loyalty to people and events that are excluded and not honoured, for example to leaders or colleagues who left the system unnoticed. If the organization doesn't respect the systemic principles, this loyalty will lead employees to set things straight, right things that are wrong. Interestingly enough, as we often reveal in a constellation, people may be totally unaware of this entanglement.

Leaders, and by extension employees, might show loyalty to another system while they are at work, exhibiting behaviour that makes sense in another context, but that is out of place in the new system. A systemic question to bring this to the surface is: 'In which system would this be normal behaviour?'

'Who or what am I loyal to?' is a critical question to ask yourself as a leader. And an additional one would be, 'What does it take to be loyal to myself?' If you are going to live and lead and relate according to your own values, you'd better be aware of what they are, where they come from, and whether they are still serving you and the people around you. Mentoring and coaching support can help you shine a light on them.

Are you willing to look at and let go of your biases?

Are you looking for confirming evidence of your own opinion? Do you want to listen to the voice of the minority or are they automatically voted out? Can you invite the wealth and possible wisdom of opposing forces? What do people see as your blind spot?

Is what you are receiving and giving really in balance (over a certain period of time) and in service of the company?

A sensitive topic that gets a lot of media coverage is whether top-level salaries and bonuses are out of control. We are not intending to open this can of worms here, but it is worth a moment of self-reflection about your own exchange.

The critical role of the integration team

> 'It's one of the characteristics of a leader that he not doubt for one moment the capacity of the people he's leading to realize whatever he's dreaming.'
> —Benjamin Zander

Benjamin Zander, the expressive musician and orchestra conductor, is well known for his live coaching sessions with musicians, in front of executive leaders. He urges them to lead in a way that brings out the full potential of people, without listening to the inner critic or igniting constant competition among the soloists and orchestra members.

How does this apply to the men and women who are tasked with the integration tactics? One of the COOs we worked with told us, 'The team you assign to a programme reflects the ambition you have for it.' Overseeing a company-wide strategic integration journey, touching many sites across the world, he witnessed some managers assigning their best resources to it, while other leaders scratched together a team. As you may expect, the tangible and intangible results reflected those managers' decisions.

It's not uncommon to see companies assigning their best strategic and technical resources to the due-diligence phase, as there is a lot to gain in that stage before putting the final bid on the table, but these people are not generally the ones in charge of the integration plans afterwards. The actual effort and time needed for integration is often underestimated. Sometimes there is a mismatch in skillsets among the integration team, sometimes the team members don't get the full attention of the leaders when raising concerns. The integration team is faced with extremely tight deadlines, which prevents members from slowing down when they need to.

Sometimes, you have to go slowly to go fast. Pausing enables the integration team members to take a balcony perspective and see the larger picture. It allows them to gain access to some deeper layers of dynamics and witness the systemic impact of certain decisions.

Many change teams only consist of members of the acquiring party, determined to complete the integration roadmap as planned, resulting in a fast but shallow integration of the new employees. The team needs to reflect the outcome that the leadership wants to achieve with the change. It is interesting to observe a large improvement initiative focused on increasing employee engagement and igniting bottom-up innovation that uses a fully structured top-down approach leaving no room for customization. It's a bit nerve-wracking to witness a PMI that was publicly positioned as building on the intrinsic strengths of both parties being led by the acquirer. That being said, it is fulfilling to work with designated change teams and look at things from their perspective. As soon as they have the insight – the 'Aha' moment – about what is making their lives so difficult and how their incorporation efforts are landing in the field, the transition to a journey of true integration and the building of a healthy new structure becomes much easier than they'd expected. Small interventions and adjustments to their tactical implementation plans make a big difference. After this process, they become convinced that the answers to their problems are present and it is just a matter of letting them emerge. As one of our coaching friends said, 'I believe the answer came along with the problem.' And sometimes a problem doesn't even demand a solution; it just wants to be seen.

Working with the integration teams is initially focused on the dynamics in the team itself, as their micro-cosmos often reflects the reality in the macro-cosmos of the organization. In exactly the same way as we do when working with executive teams or entire organizations, we apply the systemic principles to integration teams. What is their true purpose? What mandate have they been given? What is the purpose of this integration? What are some of the leading principles? Does the team have the right composition? Who belongs? Who is included? Who is excluded, but represents a critical part of the organization or a crucial quality?

What is the order in this team? Who is leading? Whose contribution is most important, and for which subjects? Note that the order can differ, depending on the work stream or topic.

What is the relevant system for each of the challenges? Is it always the entire company? Might it be one of the parties, or some departments, or a client-supplier relationship?

How does the team look at exchange? What are members bringing, and what do they expect to gain, learn or take away from this experience themselves? Have they been given enough time to really contribute? Have they been relieved from their other duties? What is the vitality in the team? Are they all exhausted and close to burnout?

Obviously, a PMI process puts a significant additional workload on the entire organization. Many integration team members also have a fully loaded day job to manage. The people under them are going through different transitional phases, with all the emotional states that come with that. It's important to keep an eye on the resilience of the leaders and the organization during the integration process. That doesn't mean you can always avoid this peak in workload, but in view of a balanced exchange, there might be other compensating mechanisms to restore balance, or at least to give people perspective.

We interviewed the CFO of a company that had just failed to complete a long-pursued acquisition. For more than a year, she'd played a key role in the negotiations and in the subsequent reconciliation between the two stubborn owners. Even though the deal was off in the end, her CEO allowed her to take a two-months paid sabbatical in appreciation of all her efforts.

Here are some useful reflection questions for the members of the integration team:

- What are you bringing (qualities, expertise, experiences) and what are you expecting to gain from being a part of this team?

- Do you have the mandate and the time to contribute fully? Are other roles, projects or tasks getting in the way of you dedicating the necessary time and attention to the integration work?

- Is the purpose of the integration and the team clear to you? Can you really connect it with your own purpose and values? If this is not the case, participants may start with good intentions, but will slack over time and lose motivation.

- Are there any (current or past, open or unspoken) conflicts between you and other key players in the integration team?

We often work with teams to establish a bystander process, one of the roles introduced by David Kantor in his book *Reading the Room*.[12] An effective bystander can intervene on a process level, signalling to the group that the discussion is getting off track, that some voices are being muted or that there is no closure on important elements. Adding a systemic lens to it, the bystander perspective warns the team when they are over-analysing, addressing symptoms or demonstrating some of the systemic dynamics themselves. This sensor capacity is vital to keep the team grounded and allow them to combine both their analytical skills and their systemic competencies.

One of our biggest sources of fulfilment is to see how people have transformed, both as individuals and as teams, at the end of the integration work. When we ask about a high point in their career, it is striking to notice how often they refer to an intense but insightful change programme, sometimes regardless of its success.

Systemic questions specific to M&As

Let's repeat some of the questions we've raised at the end of each story and explore how you might answer them differently now. We've added some questions so that you can use these lists as a reference.

Reflecting back on your previous acquisition, or considering the next one in the pipeline, consider the following:

 Purpose

- What is the strategic intent of this M&A?

- What is this M&A an excuse for?

- Which dimensions, characteristics, qualities or strengths are you trying to buy, because you lack or lost them?

- For both parties: when, how and why was this company started? Who were the founders? Who funded it?

- What were the founding principles of both?

- What is the historical timeline of both parties? What were critical milestones that have defined the company's identity?

- How can you honour the founders and the founding principles of both parties in the new narrative?

- What is the purpose of the new system?

- Are personal or financial drivers blinding the decision makers?

 Connection and inclusion:

- What determines the boundaries of the new system?

- Who and what belongs? Who and what doesn't belong any longer?

- Where do you want to be after the integration phase on the continuum from a holding structure on one end, to a fully integrated identity on the other end?

- What are the consequences of that decision for your organizational design (who belongs and needs to be included)?

- Are you planning for a hostile takeover or a real cultural integration?

- Have you evaluated the compatibility of the two cultures on a systemic level?

- What is being excluded?

- What is not supposed to be mentioned anymore?

- Are there secrets or traumatic events in the history of one or both companies?

- Who left unnoticed?

- Who still has an impact, even though they officially don't belong to the system any longer?

- If you reflect on some of the crisis situations, what are they actually masking?

 ## Order and occupying one's place:

- What is the new order of things?

- What is the new pecking order based upon?

- What is the new model for decision making? Is it transparent?

- Is the new order of things serving the new purpose?

- Are the vision, narrative and tactics cascaded down through the line to each level of the organization?

- What are your main KPIs post-merger? What has top priority? What keeps getting precedence over what and at what cost? What behaviour are you really driving with your KPIs?

- Who owns this issue (could be a trailing performance parameter, a key challenge that keeps the team awake at night, a recurring problem)?

- In which way is this issue serving the system? Is there a loyalty to something else?

- Who is authorizing your interventions?

Exchange:

- What is the new narrative? What is in it for all stakeholders?

- Who really benefits from the synergies? How about the customers?

- Who is really paying the price?

- What behaviour is rewarded here? What do you need to do to belong?

- Who or what does it serve when this does not get resolved?

- Who is giving too much?

- Who is losing in this transaction?

- What is the price of change in this company?

- What is the vitality in the organization?

A True story:
Forced Optimism

'Oh right, I shouldn't say that, we are supposed to be positive about everything lately,' she says.

The new unwritten rule is to be optimistic and under no circumstances openly challenge the bright future, strategic direction and heavily loaded implementation plans.

She is the global president of one of the major functions, has grown up in one of the merger parties and has seen it all. She is outspoken and provocative.

The two giants with a large global presence merged eighteen months ago. They were fierce competitors before; now they are supposed to get along, have each other's backs and share all their intellectual property.

Especially at the local site level and in the sales teams, people are finding that hard to swallow. The previous competitive spirit is still there; the two companies were rivals before.

'WE'RE SUPPOSED to be
POSITIVE about
EVERYTHING LATELY.'

Reflecting back on the post-integration months, she realizes that the merger has led to a vacuum in many areas. Nobody takes any decisions about the new way of working, and instead of continuing to run with the existing processes until further notice, people sit back and wait for further instructions. Now, the executives have finally defined the new corporate strategy for their function and would like to use this opportunity to move closer to one new identity.

When we review the asset footprint of the merged companies, it becomes clear that it is huge and scattered. Many of the small sites worldwide have relatively little connection to the mothership. Their identity is linked to their daily work, their location, their long-time colleagues and their original founding company – the one they started working for twenty-five or thirty years ago when the owner was present every day, walking around in worn-out boots, rolling up their sleeves and getting their hands dirty. These employees have never really started the attachment process to any of the subsequent buyers, let alone to the giant company with the two legacy names sticking uneasily to each other.

When we are reviewing the operational data, we see several anomalies, which makes us question the accuracy of the functional reporting. The numbers are out of balance; the trends in the leading indicators are not predicting the lagging ones. Our hypothesis is that the local teams are managing their shop and crew in the best way they can, independent from the corporate procedures. Only when things get out of control and they cannot hide an issue anymore will they report it.

It's a symptom of the underlying dynamics and the disconnection to the corporate approach.

We jointly define the key design criteria of the transformation the new organization requires, understanding the merged organizations' operational reality and learning from their change history. This leads us to:

- Speak the truth, allowing criticism to be expressed. No more denying of the current reality.

- The right combination of corporate topics and the freedom for local customization.

- Keep things simple and practical.

- Create visibility on the actual performance and priorities of each site.

- Support the entire integration programme with powerful and impactful communication to reach the hearts of all employees worldwide, engage them in the new narrative and connect them to the newly formed company's identity. No fancy corporate buzz-words. Clear and straightforward language.

Questions for reflection

- Which stories are being told, which ones are not to be mentioned anymore?

- What or who gets excluded?

- What are the unwritten rules in the new system?

- What were the different stages pre- and post-merger? Where are you now?

- Are there any benefits of consciously introducing a vacuum period?

- What is the right timeframe to engage the organization in the new vision and narrative?

.

8
Systemic Facilitation

'The greatest teacher, failure is.'
—Master Yoda, *Star Wars, The Last Jedi*

Setting the stage

In previous chapters, we have elaborated on the systemic principles and the beliefs, skillsets, ways of observing, working and being required to work with systemic intelligence. In the spirit of completeness, let's touch on a few facilitation skills in this chapter. Regardless of whether you are called in to support an M&A integration or to debottleneck any other business complication, these skills may well prove invaluable to you.

The attitude of the facilitator

To be a masterful systemic facilitator is to recognize in which systems we are operating and know our own systemic entanglements. The first system we get to know is the one we are born into: our family system. Pretty early on in life we become part of other systems (extended family, school, sport teams, community, early career paths, etc) and we typically don't need long to understand what it takes to belong.

One of the assignments we set for the participants in our longer systemic intelligence and organizational constellation tracks is to write a report about the dynamics in their family system and the parallels they discover in their professional life. The moment their systemic lens is activated, they find it hard *not* to see these parallels. We consider a path of personal growth as indispensable for the work we are doing. Signing up for a lifelong journey of inner work will help you to become increasingly aware of your subconscious domain, to distinguish your filters, recognize your cognitive biases and your systemic patterns.

When it comes to facilitating systemic work, we have some dos and don'ts. This is in no way a dogmatic or exhaustive list. You may want to add to it or upgrade it and make it your own.

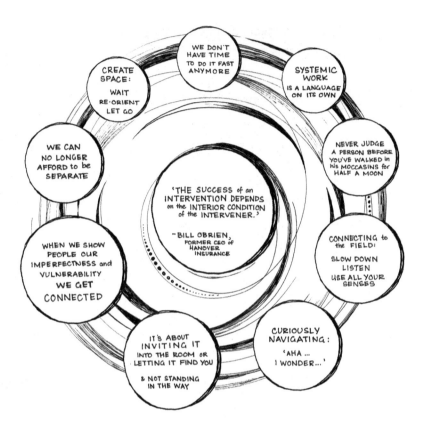

Take good care of yourself

You can only assure a high-quality presence when you are safeguarding your own wellbeing, energy level and boundaries. This is intense work. There have been many occasions in the past when we flew into a city late at night to set up the room early the next morning, spent two intense days facilitating an executive team, then ran out at the end of the two days to catch the plane to another country and another setting. Those days are mostly over. We feel an obligation to the people we are inviting into this field to show up rested and ready.

Let go of the desire to perform

It is not about you; you are serving the client's system. Approaching an organization, team, individual, recurrent issue or complex problem with systemic intelligence requires you to let go of your desired outcome, even to let go of everything you think you know. That doesn't mean that you have lost your library of wisdom and experience; it just implies that you are fully present in the moment to experience what wants to happen or be seen now. The quality of your listening deteriorates significantly if you are trying to find clues to a solution, want to be right or come across as smart.

Your need to help, fix or find solutions is not so useful. Your willingness to listen, understand, observe, witness, facilitate and resource is.

Create the right holding container

Always consider whether you have the right setting for an intervention. Don't expose a CEO in front of his or her team when they are not ready for that or when you don't have a mandate. All depends on what you have been contracted for. Being a systemic facilitator, you will obviously observe individual dynamics and possible family system entanglements, but you have not been invited to name them publicly. We cannot stress enough that it is part of your professional ethics to respect the boundaries.

When designing a longer intervention, we assure a solid forming stage in the beginning, before inviting or igniting the storming phase.

Be present from the first second

Often the first sentence in a systemic interview contains vital information. This might require you to identify your own practice or ritual to make sure you are present.

Take what people say literally, even if just for a moment

We refer to this as 'core language'. Typically, the system or the entanglements of the system are being expressed by the people, often unconsciously, so take what they say literally. Which words stay with you? Are there any statements that seem out of context or exaggerated? Pick them up and mirror them back at the right moment.

Check for permission or agreement

We find it useful to ask at the beginning what a successful first step would be. Maybe your clients only want to get a deeper insight into the situation at this moment. It may be that they want to understand what their next move should be. Respect what you have agreed to. If the opportunity arises to go one step further, check for permission again. Don't push your client unnecessarily. At each step, allow room for each person to pass or express their desire to stop.

Stick to the facts

As much as possible, only ask for facts. Since when? How many? By whom? Who made that decision? Who had the first idea? You're looking for clear, quantifiable facts. Don't allow the person you are interviewing to seduce you with stories and interpretations.

Return to the systemic questions whenever you feel you are deviating. As an example, try asking different people in the team to explain the organizational chart to you. If they all come up with a different version, or with an official one and an informal one, you know where to start. If it is difficult for you, as the facilitator, to get clarity, that may be a first indication of confusion in the system.

Don't drown in the team's stories

Stay in touch with yourself and with the team at the same time. As one of our teachers would say, 'Sit with your back against a tree.' Facilitate from that symbolic position.

Some facilitators have a stronger tendency to lean into people's stories than others. Be aware of your own patterns. Be aware of what happens in your body when you interview the client. Your body is wise and gives you signals about important remarks or references to critical events, but it requires practice and dedication to pick up those clues.

Tune in to the system

When you tune in to the entire system, rather than just the individual or team you are supporting, new insights and clarity will emerge. You will be applying active listening to the whole team, which adds another dimension.

In essence, your priority is the organizational (or family) system, not the client. That sounds strange, yet it can liberate your clients from the need to do everything on their own. Rather than making it all about them, they find their place and resources in the wider system. One of our wise colleagues, who studies Buddhist psychology, phrases it like this:

> 'If you make it all about yourself, you are making yourself more important than you actually are.'

Work with the whole system in mind, and experience how much freedom that brings.

Give direct, simple and clear instructions

Clear instructions create a safe environment; everyone understands the format. You are touching on the deep layers of the system during a constellation, which can be really intense, so it's comforting for the people you work with to trust that you, as a facilitator, are holding the structure and the process.

Some of our top team-alignment facilitation techniques introduce executives to a level of vulnerability that they are not used to. In a situation like this, we add to the psychological safety by giving clear instructions and time indications.

Please note that becoming a professional facilitator requires in-depth training and hours of observation and supervised practice. If you are not there (yet), don't hesitate to start building experience with simple constellation techniques. Ask your clients to illustrate the system and its players with objects. Stand up and let them use the room to demonstrate the relationship between the different elements. Put an illustration on the floor that represents the theme and ask the team to look at it from different angles. Moving from an intellectual analysis to a three-dimensional picture will fundamentally shift the conversation.

Small steps on a systemic level have a big impact

Less is more. Don't try to solve the world's hunger in one go.

This way of working can be overwhelming for the client. Watch them carefully. Don't force feed or share too much information, it will disturb the inner process. When you talk too much, you risk bringing them back to analysing what is going on. The effect of a systemic intervention lingers on. It is like a wave rolling on to the shore. It doesn't retreat immediately. It rolls out.

After every intervention, let go of what you know about the system

The system will shift. After every intervention, let go of your image of the system. Be willing to look at it with new eyes. Every next day is a new day, for the people you are leading and for you as a facilitator.

Suggest the team refrains from taking action right away

Often the shift has happened already. Give those waves time to roll out on the beach. As Amy Fox, Mobius' CEO, tends to say at the end of an immersive transformational leadership programme, 'In the next thirty days, don't quit your job, don't divorce your spouse, don't sell your house.'

Help the team to reorient back to the present moment

Make sure you provide proper closure for your interventions. Offer aftercare if needed.

Get supervision

Most coaches and facilitators are naturally committed to a path of growth and increased self-awareness. At the same time, many people who are attracted to these roles teach what they still struggle with themselves. Do you love facilitating difficult team dynamics, but shy away from conflict yourself? Do you urge clients to experiment with the power of a positive no, but struggle to set boundaries yourself? We know this all too well ourselves, which is why we join our own supervision circles. It allows us to explore questions or challenges that we have faced. It deepens our practice and brings our work to the next level.

Good supervision gives you the opportunity to face your shadows, pitfalls and triggers, and learn from fellow practitioners. That is why we are adamant about the need for regular supervision when you do this high-stakes and intense work.

How to influence and transform a system

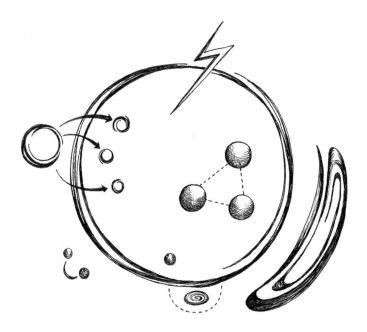

Imagine that you have concluded your diagnostics. The executive team has 'seen the light'. Together you agree on the first step. You may still be faced with a huge company, though, with multiple business units, a global footprint or a large population. Where do you start?

From a systemic point of view, a military style will not be the most effective. Force and coercion create outer compliance, but inner resistance. In some cases, they even lead to shock, trauma or complete destruction to the system. This doesn't mean you should shy away from difficult decisions or clear-cut interventions.

More effective ways to change the system sustainably are to:

Change the environment. An organizational system is not operating in isolation; there are other systems surrounding it. A system is defined by its boundaries in relation to its surroundings. If the outer layers portray an urgency to make a bold move, this will automatically influence the inner system as they interact with each other. When one element changes, there is no way that the rest can stay static.

Recommended read

An interesting read about the interconnectedness of systems with their environment is *The Bond* by Lynne McTaggart.

Find the acupuncture point. What is the smallest change that will nudge the system? Systems are very responsive to change when they are nudged in the exact right spot.

Change the rules. Create new rules; reward new behaviour. Ensure that the updated procedures, protocols and guidelines work along the systemic principles, otherwise you will be faced with new correction tactics in no time.

Seduce the system. Make it hard to resist the temptation of the new situation. In systemic work, that is often easier than you may expect. It is almost as if the whole system can ground itself again, creating on one hand a sense of relief and a moment of rest in the teams, on the other hand a renewed sense of purpose, creativity and inspiration.

Send in a Trojan horse. Let the leaders introduce the (initially) disrupting or stabilizing solution to their team first, before fully revealing what they are actually trying to achieve. One way of doing this is to take selected leaders through a deep transformative developmental experience off-site, so that they can bring the new way of being, the associated mindset and tools back to the system themselves.

Create pockets of change within the system and connect them to multiply the impact. Create systemic change champions or departments. Focus on current and future leaders who will drive the systemic transformation. They can lead pilot areas or departments that will attract the attention of other units and can act as a lighthouse.

Introduce new leaders/new talent. These people can bring in fresh insights and are not contaminated by the old ways of working. In some situations, you will need a critical mass of fresh blood to inject energy into a team or a site that is close to burnout or doesn't have the capacity to adapt to the new.

Beware, though: all of these tactics can fail when the underlying dynamics are not tackled. Despite a crystal-clear business case and a well-designed implementation strategy, an organizational system can silently sabotage everything you want to achieve.

The knowing field

> 'Unfortunately, no one can be told what the matrix is. You have to see it for yourself.'
> —Morpheus, from the movie *The Matrix*

A chapter about systemic facilitation would not be complete without touching on the notion of the knowing field, but we will not describe it in too many words as it makes more sense to let you experience it yourself.

Rewind to physics lessons in high school, the teacher telling you the definition of a force field – a vector field indicating the forces exerted by one object on another. This force field is there in each contact between two people; in a team; in leaders' interactions with their people; between a client and a supplier. If we could see it, it would provide us with a lot of information about the interdependencies in a system. What is the nature of the connections? How strong are they? What is the chain of events?

In constellation work, we use the knowing field to identify what is really going on. What are the invisible currents that make us drift away from our purpose? How can we discern between the symptoms and the real dynamics at play? Thinking in terms of a field helps us to move our focus from the problem to the relationship a client has with the problem.

By engaging with the field, we are translating the two-dimensional view on the situation to a three-dimensional perspective. Even asking someone to demonstrate using the water glasses and salt and pepper shakers on the table makes that additional dimension visible.

For us – as leaders, facilitators, consultants and coaches – to connect to that field, we need to go beyond listening and analysing with our eyes and ears. We use our entire body and the sensitivity of our nervous system to give us additional information and hints about what is really going on and what the next question or next step could be.

We invite you to start experimenting with this myste-
rious field.

A True Story: Triangulation

She exhibits the newspaper articles on the table in front of us:

'End of nasty divorce between company x and company y'

'Company x cashes millions of euros to end the "packaging" war'

'Packaging war between x and y gets (temporary?) resolution'

She feels worn out after years of hard labour to make this 50/50 joint venture work, first in her role as legal counsel to the CEO of one company during the contracting phase, later – when the frictions reached a peak – as a designated strategic advisor between both parties.

Her home company is a manufacturing company: family-owned, listed on the local stock market, with seven production facilities in different countries, currently led by two brothers. The other party's CEO/founder never aspired to produce: in his family business he leads a team of inventors focused on developing innovative packaging prototypes.

One of their promising inventions excites the brothers, as this environmentally friendly solution would boost their sustainability aspirations. After signing the joint venture deal, they soon find out that the solution is in an early stage and needs another two years of technical development and scale-up. Despite the 50/50 ownership, they are the ones investing, which does not mean the other CEO plays second fiddle. He is omnipresent, loud and overrules critical decisions. Trust between both parties is low from the start.

The joint venture organization lacks structure, leadership and a location. People assigned to it are spread all over, mostly at different production facilities (company x). The management meetings are held in the inventor's office (company y). The strategic advisor is considered by both parties to be a trustworthy person, so she is asked to step in and bring order. She is constantly building bridges between the two CEOs.

Listening, soothing, finding compromises, going back and forth.

We explain to her the dynamic of triangulation, when someone gets pulled in a conflict between two parties higher up in the order – like a child who is mediating between their two parents. She sighs. This is exactly what she has experienced during the last two years.

When we fast-forward to the press coverage from the last few days, we ask her what happened in the end that led to the divorce. It turns out that the inventor CEO had been silently courting an external investor. He wants to take full ownership over the product and its future, even though he doesn't have the capacity and manufacturing experience to do so. An intense period of fighting has just been concluded with a financial deal.

There is relief and also mourning. The brothers believed in the solution and jumped through hoops to solve every roadblock along the way. They actively engage in a post-mortem analysis as a team: naming what is, honouring the contribution of all involved, connecting to both the learnings and the loss.

As we continue our chat, we ask her about the two brothers. She talks almost solely about one of them during our conversation and we are curious about the younger brother. She explains that they had decided from the start that one of them would take the lead in this joint venture, so that the other brother could focus on the day-to-day operation.

But as she reflects on it, she realizes that she recalls numerous times over the years that she worked for them when she was mediating between the two brothers. She seemed to be the only one who could calm them down when one of them would explode and they were not talking.

'Triangulation?' she asks.

A few days later she gives us a call. She has reflected on the systemic principles as they play out in both family systems and organizational systems. We talk about the fact that family businesses are faced with the challenge of overlapping systems and multiple entanglements.

'I was wondering,' she says, 'the two brothers had a middle sister. She died more than twenty years ago. Could that be related to my role?'

Questions for reflection

- What is your experience with a shared ownership or 50/50 collaboration?

- What do both parties bring and what do they gain with the joint venture?

- With two captains on one ship, what are the underlying criteria for order?

- How would you describe some of the dynamics in your family of origin? What are the key messages that have been repeated over and over again, spoken or unspoken? What does it take to belong?

- Which of the dynamics in your family system do you recognize in your professional environment?

- What is your true story?

9
Spin-Offs And Mergers On A Smaller Scale

'Every moment was a precious thing, having in it
the essence of finality.'
—Daphne du Maurier

Setting the stage

A book about M&As is incomplete without including
the opposite movement. Having lived through several
divestitures and spin-offs, and currently supporting clients in the formation of separate business units, we also
use the systemic lens to look at a 'divorce'. We are determined to make it an amicable one for both the original
company, which changes shape with the departure of
one of its businesses, and the unit that leaves.

We have seen many different scenarios.

For the divesting party

- Companies mourning the loss of what were once their 'crown jewels' or their foundational products or services

- Companies feeling relieved to be free from the burden of a systemically underperforming business unit

- Business units wondering whether they will be the next ones that have to go

- People or teams envious of the ones who left, as they were acquired by a more attractive party

- Leaders immediately looking for the next merger or acquisition to restore the original size of the company

For the divested party

- An immediate shift to an 'us versus them' mentality

- A feeling of having been the unwanted child in the previous family (and being better off now)

- Excitement to take the future in their own hands

- Mourning the loss of the previous identity

- Maintaining a strong connection to the previous owner and the colleagues they left behind

- An initial honeymoon feeling as the new buyer or partner has big investment plans for them

- The feeling of being set up for failure by the original company (leaving with a burden of liability or debt)

- A rapid decline in the actualization of the core values

Luckily, we also see well-managed identity shifts, where purpose is thoroughly redefined, leading to a real turnaround and longer-term success.

How can the four systemic principles guide us during these multiple separation transitions? When the divestiture or spin-off is sold to or forming a partnership with a new party, everything we said in the previous chapters applies to this merger or acquisition. Let's now look at the scenario of a standalone or spinoff and list the systemic questions for both parties.

 ## Purpose for both parties

For the original company

- How is this divestiture serving your purpose?

- Was it unavoidable?

- What is this divestiture an excuse for? What are the problems that you are not facing, or have not been able to resolve, so you assume this divestiture to be the best or only solution?

- How does this shift in your composition, size and shape influence your identity?

- Do you need to rethink your purpose?

- Will you be missing critical elements or qualities after the departure?

- Will you allow the leaving business or unit a fair chance to survive and thrive? What is the burden you are putting on it?

For the standalone or spin-off business

- What is the new purpose of your standalone unit or business?

- Has it shifted?

- How do you rally the organization around the (new) purpose, now that the employees don't belong to a bigger whole any longer?

- What are the guiding principles? Which ones do you take along from the previous company? Which ones do you leave behind because they no longer serve your redefined purpose?

Connection and inclusion for both parties

For the original company

- How can you say goodbye to the ones leaving – the people, the products, the expertise and qualities, the brands?

- How can you avoid the employees who stay feeling that a part of their identity has left?

- What are the rituals to assure a proper ending so that both companies can embark on a new journey?

- How can you honour the contribution to the organization of the leaving business and its people, even if it has been loss-making in the last years?

- How can you include the feelings of mourning and loss? Some of your people may have been a part of building that business in the first place.

- How can you reconnect the entire organization to the new or renewed purpose?

For the standalone or spin-off business

- How can you say goodbye to the original company?

- How can you bow to what it has given you (resources, investment, experience, learnings), even if you feel undervalued, underinvested in, dismissed or rejected?

- What are the rituals to allow you to move on as a separate entity without rejecting the original 'parent' company? You are metaphorically cutting the umbilical cord.

- How can you include the feelings of mourning and loss that will be a natural part of the separation process?

- What needs to be included and what needs to be left behind?

- How do you rally the troops around the new purpose? What is it that will connect them to the new?

 ## Order and occupying one's place for both parties

For the original company

- What are the criteria to establish the new order, focused on achieving the renewed purpose?

- How do you fill the missing positions?

- How do you set the new leaders up for success?

- How do you avoid people remaining attached to the leaders who left the company?

- What is the new or reshuffled order and contribution to the organization of the remaining businesses? The previous second largest may become the largest as of now. A spin-off may call for a rearrangement of some of the business units that were sourcing the one that left.

For the standalone or spin-off business

- A new start offers the opportunity to rethink the criteria to establish the order. Is what was true in the original company still true now?

- What does the order need to be based on?

- How do you choose the new leader and their team?

- What are the criteria that will make the standalone company successful? How do you bring the right people in to make it happen?

- How can you be fully transparent about it (as people may assume the old is still valid)?

- How much empowerment can you cascade down through the line? We have recently supported a spin-off where the change team repeated over and over again that the new company would be able to take the future in its own hands. Is that true? Can you make that a reality, even in harsh business conditions?

Exchange for both parties

A spin-off implies a significant amount of work from all employees. Organizations and teams need to be identified and assigned to one company or the other, assets need to be split, systems have to be disentangled, service-level agreements may be needed for common utilities or real estate. A lot is being asked from people.

On top of that, most people will feel that things have been taken away from them – for example, an identity, status, belonging to a brand name, longstanding colleagues, a well-known work location, a set of established compensation benefits, a specific way of working. You name it.

Also, the people in the original company are losing colleagues and friends, a shared history, the common stories of failure and success. In addition to this, they may also lose a certain level of service they are used to as functions downsize, given that they are now effectively providing services to a smaller organization. Exchange is a critical principle to watch during this transition.

For the original company

- What is the extra workload pre- and post-spin-off?

- How do you keep an eye on what you are asking from people?

- What could be some of the compensating mechanisms?

- How do you allow the feeling of 'something being taken away' to be expressed?

- How are you fully transparent about what is about to change, which of the processes or services will be re-engineered, and why?

For the standalone or spin-off business

- How do you identify and communicate the win-win in this transaction?

- How will you be fully transparent about the new reality, even when there is a lot of loss in it?

- How do you search for and value other traits: new opportunities; more autonomy; the challenge to turn a business around; more influence on the decision making; learning from new people?

- How do you find compensating mechanisms to ease the transition without making them eternal privileges?

We recently worked with a company that compensated the move to a new location, following a spin-off, by allowing people to work from home three days a week. The offices were still largely empty now, even though this transition happened fifteen years ago and there were only a few people left from those days.

All new employees had stepped into a 'two-days-in-the-office' right that was not supporting the cross-functional learning and collaboration needed now.

In our experience, the systemic principles and the lens to recognize symptoms and understand the deeper dynamics at play have been as helpful in divestitures and spin-offs as in M&As. By extension, they are invaluable in any complex business challenge or navigating any organizational or societal system. This approach will support you in identifying the most urgent and impactful interventions on a deeper level.

Mergers on a smaller scale

The systemic lens and principles apply to different scales of M&As; to various forms of integration efforts; to mergers of departments and teams; to partnerships between companies across the value chain. This way of working often reveals the actual rationale behind the growth strategy; it brings the invisible connections to the surface; it unmasks the true nature of both cultures, which allows us to identify the most effective approach and interventions to accelerate the integration and set teams up for long-term success.

With this in mind, we added small and medium-sized companies (SMEs) to our research. We looked at family-owned companies that ran their heads into the wall once or twice and learned from it to redefine their inorganic growth plans. We examined SMEs that merged their talents and intellectual property in a partnership, aimed at approaching the market with one combined value proposition and one voice. We even saw parallel processes and dynamics in the fusion of two townships and their struggle to merge their policies and approach to indoor and outdoor sport facilities for their citizens.

One specific type of SME is the family business. Family businesses are a clear yet complex example of entangled systems. As much as the owners or managers may claim they are separating their business from their family life, it is unavoidable that the dynamics in the family system will sneak into the business.

We have observed the dynamics in a small construction firm, where the husband takes on the CEO role and his wife leads HR. As a result, critical issues are often not raised by employees, leading them to fester until it is almost too late to intervene.

If you are leading or consulting with family businesses, we advise you to learn more about family systemic work, as all your other efforts may fail if you don't understand and tackle the entanglements there. Ask yourself what the relevant system is for the theme you are working on.

A large percentage of global revenue is generated by SMEs as they assure the majority of the world's employment, so it is essential to provide them with the map and the compass to find their way to sustainable growth.

Afterword

'What is the relevant system for this question?'

Even though we uphold that it is important to define the relevant system for each of our interventions and for each of your challenges – whether it is a team, a department, the entire company, the supplier-client relationship, the community interaction, the larger value chain, etc – if we reflect on the true meaning of purpose, and if we are serious about long-term sustainability, shouldn't we conclude that there is only one relevant system? Namely the natural system that is the source of everything. Can we ever create value when we are depleting our natural resources, destroying our environment, or exploiting humanity? Is it possible to be a value-driven and ethical leader, employee, consultant or coach, striving to improve business performance and serve customer needs, without asking ourselves some deep existential questions about how we impact the world?

It is critical to stay in the game and raise the bar, set new rules, bring in a higher consciousness and choose to operate from within.

Having worked in the chemical, medical and pharmaceutical industry, and with companies and leaders in mining, metals, food, retail, fast-moving consumer goods, shipping and transportation, pulp and paper, financial services and banking, and education, we see ethical leaders grasping the huge challenges they have in front of them as part of a specific industry and reflecting on their own past contributions to many of the problems.

The food industry, originally purposed to provide affordable food for a growing world population, is facing a range of massive challenges: food waste; the use of hazardous chemicals in the processing of food or in fertilizing the land; the loss of nutritional value in most of our fast food and the consequences for our health; the environmental impact of herding cattle for human consumption or cutting down the rainforest; the harsh conditions for the animals we eat, etc. The pharmaceutical industry is finding life-saving cures for terrible diseases, but has at the same time played a significant role in the opioids crisis. On a deeper systemic level, the banking industry doesn't seem to have learned enough from the 2008 crisis.

All industries and corporations are facing major challenges, as stipulated in the UN's Sustainable Development Goals:[13]

- Child labour

- Emissions into water, soil and air

- Depletion of the rain forest

- Extracting oil in the natural habitat of fauna and flora threatened with extinction

- Plastic waste in our oceans

- Overproduction and overconsumption

- Highly hazardous waste

- Entire communities living below the poverty threshold

- Workplace fatalities and catastrophic accidents

- Global warming

- Segregated education

- Third-party risk

The list is endless.

Maybe the quest is to bring humanity back to our corporate world. How can we all – leaders, influencers, employees, consultants, coaches, diplomats, political leaders and consumers – respect the true natural principles of living systems?

Notes

1   The article Goold, M; Campbell A (October 1998)
    'Desperately Seeking Synergy'. *Harvard Business
    Review*. https://hbr.org/1998/09/desperately-
    seeking-synergy points at the synergy bias of
    many corporate executives.

2   Kengelbach, J; Berberich, U; Keienburg, G
    (October 2015) 'Why Deals Fail'. *Boston Consulting
    Group*. www.bcg.com/publications/2015/why-
    deals-fail.aspx

    Fuhrer, C; Liem, R; Zwald, D (2017) *PwC's M&A
    Integration Survey Report: Success Factors in Post-
    merger Integration: Deal makers share their recipes for
    success*. PwC. www.pwc.de/de/deals/success-
    factors-in-post-merger-integration.pdf

Kautzsch, T; Thomählen, H (2015) *Post-merger Integration: A tailored approach to sustainable transaction success.*

3   Deutsch, C; West, A (2010) *A New Generation of M&A: A McKinsey perspective on the opportunities and challenges.* McKinsey & Company https://tinyurl.com/yb55f57n

4   Kengelbach et al (2015) 'Why Deals Fail' (see note 2).

5   Kiely, D (June 2018) 'Don't Neglect Your Customers During a Merger'. *Harvard Business Review* https://hbr.org/2018/06/dont-neglect-your-customers-during-a-merger

6   Regis, R; Kloubek, A; Ojha, S(2016) *Post-merger Integration Planning.* EXL. www.exlservice.com/resources/assets/library/documents/EXL_WP_Post_merger_integration_planning.pdf

7   Fuhrer et al (2017) *PwC's M&A Integration Survey Report* (see note 2).

8   Deutsch and West (2010) *A New Generation of M&A* (see note 3).

9   Kautzsch and Thomählen (2015) Post-merger Integration (see note 2).

10 See the bibliography at the end of the book for details of publications that have inspired us on this journey.

11 Berlow, E (2014) 'Simplifying Complexity'. https://youtu.be/UB2iYzKeej8

12 Kantor, D (2012) *Reading the Room: Group dynamics for coaches and leaders*. San Francisco, CA: Jossey-Bass.

13 See www.un.org/sustainabledevelopment/ sustainable-development-goals

Bibliography

Publications referenced

Bourton, S; Lavoie, J; Vogel, T (March 2018) 'Leading with Inner Agility'. *McKinsey & Company Quarterly.* www.mckinsey.com/business-functions/organization/our-insights/leading-with-inner-agility McKinsey & Company

Deutsch, C; West, A (2010) *A New Generation of M&A: A McKinsey perspective on the opportunities and challenges.* McKinsey & Company. https://tinyurl.com/y3hvrtvb

Fuhrer, C; Liem, R; Zwald, D (2017) *PwC's M&A Integration Survey Report: Success Factors in Post-merger Integration: Deal makers share their recipes for success'*. www.pwc.de/de/deals/success-factors-in-post-merger-integration.pdf PWC

Gass, R (2010) *What is Transformational Change?* http://hiddenleaf.electricembers.net/wp-content/uploads/2010/06/What-is-Transformational-Change.pdf

Goold, M; Campbell, A (October 1998) 'Desperately Seeking Synergy'. *Harvard Business Review.* https://hbr.org/1998/09/desperately-seeking-synergy

Kautzsch, T; Thomählen, H (2015) *Post-merger Integration: A tailored approach to sustainable transaction success.* Oliver Wyman. www.oliverwyman.com/content/dam/oliver-wyman/global/en/files/archive/2005/Post_Merger_Integration.pdf

Kengelbach, J; Berberich, U; Keienburg, G (October 2015) 'Why Deals Fail'. Boston Consulting Group. www.bcg.com/publications/2015/why-deals-fail.aspx

Kiely, D (June 2018) 'Don't Neglect Your Customers During a Merger'. *Harvard Business Review.* https://hbr.org/2018/06/dont-neglect-your-customers-during-a-merger

Regis, R; Kloubek, A; Ojha, S (2016) *Post-merger Integration Planning.* EXL. www.exlservice.com/

resources/assets/library/documents/EXL_WP_
Post_merger_integration_planning.pdf

Snowden, DJ; Boone, ME (November 2007) 'A
Leader's Framework for Decision Making'. *Harvard
Business Review*. https://hbr.org/2007/11/a-leaders-
framework-for-decision-making

Books that inspired us

Bridges, W (2017) *Managing Transitions: Making the
most of change*. Philadelphia, PA: Da Capo Press

Collins, JC (2001) *Good to Great: Why some companies make the leap… and others don't*. New York:
HarperCollins Publishers

Collins, JC; Porras, JI (1994) *Built to Last: Successful
habits of visionary companies*. New York: HarperCollins
Publishers

de Geus, A (1997) *The Living Company: Habits for survival in a turbulent business environment*. Cambridge,
MA: Harvard Business School

Fox, EA (2013) *Winning from Within: A breakthrough
method for leading, living and lasting change*. New York,
HarperCollins Publishers

Franke, U (2005) *In My Mind's Eye: Family constellations in individual therapy and counselling.* Heidelberg: Carl Auer International

Garvey Berger, J (2019) *Unlocking Leadership Mindtraps: How to thrive in complexity.* Stanford, CA: Stanford University Press

Garvey Berger, J; Johnston, K (2015) *Simple Habits for Complex Times: Powerful practices for leaders.* Stanford, CA: Stanford University Press

Jaworski, J (2003) *Synchronicity: The inner path of leadership.* San Francisco, CA: Berret-Koehler Publishers

Kantor, D (2012) *Reading the Room: Group dynamics for coaches and leaders.* San Francisco, CA: Jossey-Bass

Kegan, R (1998) *In Over Our Heads: The mental demands of modern life.* Cambridge MA: Harvard University Press

Laloux, F (2014) *Reinventing Organizations: A guide to creating organizations inspired by the next stage of human consciousness.* Brussels: Nelson Parker

Lewin, K (1997) *Resolving Social Conflicts: Field theory in social science.* Washington, DC: American Psychological Association

Maturana, H; Varela, F (1980) *Autopoiesis and Cognition: The realization of the living*. Boston, MA: D. Reidel Publishing Company

McChrystal, General S (2015) *Teams of Teams: New rules of engagement for a complex world*. New York: Penguin Publishing Group

McTaggart, L (2011) *The Bond: Connecting through the space between us*. London: Hay House UK ltd

Rosselet, C; Senoner, G (201) *Enacting Solutions: Management Constellations: An innovative approach to problem-solving and decision-making in organizations*. Milan: Edizioni Ledizioni LediPublishing

Rowling, JK (2003) *Harry Potter and the Order of the Phoenix*. London: Bloomsbury Publishing

Scharmer, O (2016) *Theory U: Leading from the future as it emerges*. San Francisco, CA: Berret-Koehler Press

Schmidt, JB (2006) *Inner Navigation: Traumahealing and constellation process work as navigation tools for the evolution of your true self*. Hamburg: Aptitude-Academy

Senge, P (1990) *The Fifth Discipline: The art and practice of the learning organization*. New York: Doubleday

Senge, P; Jaworski, J; Scharmer, O; Flowers, BS (2005) *Presence: Human purpose and the field of the future.* Boston, MA: Nicholas Brealy Publishing

Sparrer, I (2007) *Miracle, Solution and System: Solution-focused systemic structural constellations for therapy and organisational change.* Cheltenham: SolutionsBooks

Stam, JJ (2006) *Fields of Connection: The practice of organizational constellations.* Groningen: Het Noorderlicht

Stam JJ (2016) *Wings for Change: Systemic organizational development.* Groningen: Het Noorderlicht

Whittington, J (2012) *Systemic Coaching and Constellations: An introduction to the principles, practices and application.* London: Kogan Page Limited

TED talks that inspired us

Berlow, E (2014) 'Simplifying Complexity'. https://youtu.be/UB2iYzKeej8

Zander, B (2008) 'The Transformative Power of Classical Music'. https://youtu.be/r9LCwI5iErE

Acknowledgements

Sharing is growing. On this lifelong learning voyage, we are just one unique knot in a colourful, interconnected and interwoven tapestry of teachers.

We would like to honour our loving support network, the bright minds and souls who have influenced us and brought us to this moment in time.

Mieke

Dedicated to my beautiful children Marie and Nicolas, who are gracefully navigating in different systems. Who will you become?

To Matthew Myers: for our endless poetic conversations. For your great gift of increasing my presence, by aligning my body, mind and soul. For our love.

Paul

Dedicated to my wife and soulmate Anita, who knows and shows love like only she can.

To my two wise kids, Yaron and Leah, who teach me about life every day.

On behalf of both authors

We would like to acknowledge our constellation and systemic intelligence lineage:

- Bouke de Boer, a teacher and a friend. The man who introduced Paul to family systems and the force and possibilities of working at deeper levels to help heal systems.

- Johannes Schmidt, with whom Paul explored the first steps into organizational constellations and many other forms of systemic work.

- Jaap van der Wal, whose work on 'embryosophy' demonstrates how everything is a repetition of what we've learned in the womb, and therefore of life in its essence.

- Jan Jacob Stam, a fellow organizational constellator who brought us the fourth principle of purpose and showed how organizational constellations have their own dynamics, different from family systems.

- Carola Castillo, who is always looking for the next new edge in systemic work. Her work on Reconstructive® is truly a source of inspiration.

- Mathias Varga von Kibed and Insa Sparrer, the developers of Syst® systemic structural constellations. They are pioneers, experimenting and bringing different fields of knowledge together.

- Daan van Kampenhout, who taught us to see the larger fields, all generations, long lineages and dynamics in large groups and cultures. He initiated the inclusion of the practices of native peoples as part of our work.

- Bertus Gazenbeek, who made us remember that every system is also represented in us. Who as a constellator is in total service to the one(s) in need.

- Annamaria Bosmans, who brings the gentle and determined wisdom from the elders through family and dream constellations and with the horses of Miradal.

- Martin Breed, with whom Paul spent thousands of hours debating and challenging the systemic principles in the reality of work. A true systemic manager.

- Eric Souren, a dear friend and 24/7 sojourner, who invited Mieke on the path of systemic and constellation work with a seemingly-innocent question: 'Where were you sitting at the dinner table as a child?'

Our Mobius lineage:

- Amy Elizabeth Fox, Mobius's founder and CEO, a visionary master of many worlds, a tireless connector of conscious souls, and a powerful manifestor of her dream to call upon a different reality and lead from a position of love.

- Erica Ariel Fox, Mobius's chief thought leader and *New York Times* best-selling author of *Winning from Within*™, who never ceases to expand our view on what is possible when we witness how she masters her force field to enable true breakthroughs with senior leaders.

- Jennifer Garvey Berger: her work and passion for adult development and leading in complexity inspired us to keep looking for simple solutions in the complexity of M&As and divestitures.

- Jen Cohen, who taught us how events and trauma get stored in the body. This helped us to recognize the same phenomena in the tissue of an organization.

- Alexander Caillet, top team coaching expert, founder of Corentus and our dear friend, who never ceases to challenge us and with whom we love to dance.

Our mystical lineage:

- Thomas Hübl, who reminds us that holding on to a younger version of ourselves is no longer enough. Who invites us to be global social witnesses in service to our currently fragmented world and to engage with collective trauma on a deeper level.

- Hans van den Braak, Mieke's holistic doctor and visionary guide for thirty years, who passed away in 2016 and is still missed.

And a special thank you to:

- Rosi Greenberg for her beautiful artwork, for bringing our stories to life in her drawings.

- Josephine Schoolkate for considerate yet straightforward feedback, for multifaceted referencing to other business books, for her endorsement.

- Yaron Zonneveld for smart, thoughtful and humorous proofreading and editing. You took this request from your father seriously and your input has been invaluable to us.

- Tim Andrews, who savoured our words and highlighted the marketing potential of specific sentences. He is a lifelong friend, a true guide and companion.

- Eva Hernandez, who confirmed to us the opposite forces that are often at play on a macro-economic level. We share a desire to include the long-term sustainability of organizations and the wellbeing of all people involved.

- Martijn Barnas, who challenged us with thorough feedback. His reflections were an important test for us and helped us to stay true to the book that we wanted to write.

We would like to thank:

- All the clients we've worked with in the last twenty-five years and the people we interviewed for this book who trusted us with their memories. You are all human beings, of flesh and blood. These are your real struggles. We hope we do your passion and commitment justice with our words.

- You – the readers, future clients or thought leaders – for your trust in us.

Finally, we would like to thank the many beautiful souls who have crossed our paths, influenced our lives, dared to trust us and believe in our work. We can't even start to count all the scary and daring moments when you stood at our side, willing to love us, no matter what.

The Authors

Mieke Jacobs

Based in Belgium, Mieke has more than twenty years of industrial experience. She has been involved in several strategic shifts in Fortune 100 companies, including global operational excellence and transformational change programmes, and the entrance into new or adjacent industries through mergers and acquisitions.

She has also been a global leader in operations management consulting. She has travelled the world, acting as a strategic advisor and thought leader to industry-leading global companies in multiple industries, including oil and gas, chemicals, manufacturing, pharma, utilities, distribution, fast-moving consumer goods and the food industry. Her work has focused on strategic change journeys, value protection and value creation.

She is now an international consultant, facilitator and coach to executive teams, and a senior consultant and faculty member for Mobius Executive Leadership. Together with Paul, she teaches international masterclasses in Boston and Amsterdam on systemic intelligence and organizational constellations.

She has a passion for people and organizational dynamics, and has acquired skills and certifications in this area. She applies all these insights in her facilitation and transformation work with leaders, teams and organizations.

She is a thought leader, having authored several articles and white papers, and has been a passionate keynote speaker at conferences across the globe. Her lifelong love for writing has resulted in her first book, a novel based on systemic work, published in February 2017.

She holds a Master's degree in economics/engineering from the University of Leuven in Belgium and the University of Bilbao in Spain.

Paul Zonneveld

 Based in Amsterdam, Paul is a Mobius Executive Leadership senior faculty for top team interventions and an executive coach, with over twenty-five years of international business experience in various roles. He has unique expertise in understanding systems, enabling him to offer insight into how to manage change and transformation for leaders of large companies, those who find themselves in complex situations or those going through M&A.

Today, Paul focuses on supporting professionals and leaders to connect with their internal leadership qualities, such as self-awareness, courage and balance, and how to invite these qualities in others around them. He also teaches system sensibility – system awareness – to enable leaders to work effectively with the deeper dynamics driving their businesses.

Paul is the programme director and leading trainer at various training institutes, teaching the use of systemic intelligence in coaching and how to apply it to complex organizational topics. He is a member of the Dutch association of organizational experts and advisors and an internationally certified trainer. He actively supports the Muses foundation, helping young adults creating a more sustainable world through social and development aid in 'underprivileged' regions in the world.

Contact

🌐 http://thepowerofsystemicintelligence.com

✉ Mieke.Jacobs@mobiusleadership.com

✉ Paul.Zonneveld@mobiusleadership.com

Lightning Source UK Ltd.
Milton Keynes UK
UKHW020251131219
355185UK00007B/158/P